I0110557

HOME MANAGEMENT

Rupa Chatterjee

V&S PUBLISHERS

Published by:

V&S PUBLISHERS

F-2/16, Ansari road, Daryaganj, New Delhi-110002
☎ 23240026, 23240027 • *Fax:* 011-23240028
Email: info@vspublishers.com • *Website:* www.vspublishers.com

Regional Office : Hyderabad
5-1-707/1, Brij Bhawan (Beside Central Bank of India Lane)
Bank Street, Koti, Hyderabad - 500 095
☎ 040-24737290
E-mail: vspublishershyd@gmail.com

Branch Office : Mumbai
Jaywant Industrial Estate, 1st Floor–108, Tardeo Road
Opposite Sobo Central Mall, Mumbai – 400 034
☎ 022-23510736
E-mail: vspublishersmum@gmail.com

Follow us on:

© **Copyright:** V&S PUBLISHERS
Edition 2018

DISCLAIMER

While every attempt has been made to provide accurate and timely information in this book, neither the author nor the publisher assumes any responsibility for errors, unintended omissions or commissions detected therein. The author and publisher makes no representation or warranty with respect to the comprehensiveness or completeness of the contents provided.

All matters included have been simplified under professional guidance for general information only, without any warranty for applicability on an individual. Any mention of an organization or a website in the book, by way of citation or as a source of additional information, doesn't imply the endorsement of the content either by the author or the publisher. It is possible that websites cited may have changed or removed between the time of editing and publishing the book.

Results from using the expert opinion in this book will be totally dependent on individual circumstances and factors beyond the control of the author and the publisher.

It makes sense to elicit advice from well informed sources before implementing the ideas given in the book. The reader assumes full responsibility for the consequences arising out from reading this book.

For proper guidance, it is advisable to read the book under the watchful eyes of parents/guardian. The buyer of this book assumes all responsibility for the use of given materials and information.

The copyright of the entire content of this book rests with the author/publisher. Any infringement/transmission of the cover design, text or illustrations, in any form, by any means, by any entity will invite legal action and be responsible for consequences thereon.

Contents

■■

Preface

Management has become a key element of modern life. Whether in office or factories, commercial businesses or the hotel industry, systems have been developed to ensure the smooth and efficient functioning of any organization. Since this is so, why should the home which is the first and primary unit of organization be left behind? There is a need to organize the home front so that we are able to function efficiently when we step outside its doors.

Why should the home, which is the primary and most important unit of society be left outside its purview? If men, women and children are to reach their work place and schools or colleges on time, they need to be properly clothed, fed and rested in order to perform effectively. Since modern life proceeds at an unrelenting pace and time is a precious commodity, there is a need to systematize our activities.

For centuries, the role played by the homemaker—wife, mother and housewife has not been adequately appreciated. This job receives no monetary remuneration, there are no prescribed working hours and often the housewife downplays her role by saying, "I am just a housewife". This is a sad spillover from the success-driven, money chasing Western norms that are invading our society. In keeping society healthy, happy, well-nourished and balanced, the home manager and home management plays a pivotal role, since she is called upon to be a chef, a financial wizard, an interior decorator, a doctor, a nurse, a psychologist, a wife, mother, daughter-in-law, friend and social worker—all rolled into one!

I strongly believe that the homemaker/housewife plays an invaluable role. For example, the child or teenager who is given nutritious and lovingly prepared food at home, will not be forced to live on a diet of fast food which leads to obesity and also malnutrition on account of the empty calories present in the food. In fact, Dr. Jyoti Sharma in an article entitled "Straight To His Stomach" published in the September 2000 issue of *"Woman's Era"* magazine goes so far as to say, "What ails Western society is lack of cooking skills" as she noticed that in Frankfurt, Germany, ..."women do not cook there. They survive on canned food, or they buy fast food."

There is much more to home management than cooking although this is undoubtedly an important ingredient in building up a happy home. I have tried to touch upon all aspects that contribute towards the running of a household, which unlike an office is a twenty-four hour, endless assignment. The cycle of cooking-cleaning-washing clothes-washing dishes-ironing clothes-putting them away is never ending. In order to eliminate the twin phrases of 'harried' and 'harum scarum' housewife, I have tried to introduce systems into every sphere of housekeeping so that the house runs efficiently.

I hope this book will be of practical use to both young girls who are expecting to set up house, as well as to experienced homemakers who may also find some of the information innovative. I also hope that this volume will bring a greater understanding and respect for the many hours of continuous hard work that goes into the running of a well-managed household.

—Rupa Chatterjee
July 1, 2001

CHAPTER-1

Home Management — A Necessity

If management is the key to modern life, why should the home and household be left behind? As modern life hurtles along at an unrelenting pace, people find that they have endless chores to be done, but hardly any time to do them. Moreover, there is no longer a clear division between men and women into breadwinners and homemakers.

There are many types of households today—there may be a traditional household, a double income household, a nuclear household, a modern joint family, a traditional joint family, a single person household or a single parent household. However, the bottom line in all these set-ups remains the same—the house or household has to be managed and all activities have to be organised in a systematic way if the members are to lead happy and efficient lives. Household work is of an unending nature—meals have to be prepared, clothes and dishes have to be washed, shopping done, milk, water have to be boiled and beds made. Once the chores are done, the cycle starts again, with the chores being done once or even several times a day. In those households where there are servants, things may function more effortlessly, but it nevertheless devolves on the housewife to streamline all activities into an efficient system so that all members of the household function effectively. How can one go to office or school without meals being cooked and eaten, clothes washed and ironed, beds made and adequate rest taken in congenial environment? Some one, therefore, has to manage the home, whether it is in a remote village, a small town, a metropolis or amidst palatial surroundings. Budgets and needs may vary, food habits may differ but the necessity for home management cannot be denied. In an increasingly systems-oriented world, there is today a need to understand and appreciate the value of home management. What is unique about household management is that all chores have to be done so routinely and repetitively, that there is little appreciation for all the planning and hard work that has preceded the smooth functioning. Only when there are no meals, no clean clothes, and no well-maintained household that one realises the chaos that results from a disorganised home. Hence, home management is essential to ensure a smooth and well run household in which all members are able to function efficiently outside the home.

Organising the Household

Having pervaded every sphere of modern life, the home cannot get exempted from the purview of management. Every housewife is a manager in an unpaid, unofficial capacity and irrespective of whether the setting is rural or urban, it is evident that every household has a domestic management routine. For example, a housewife in rural India would count getting water from the well, milking the cows and lighting the "chullah" as part of her early morning chores. The urban housewife on the other hand, may just have to press a switch to

start the water pump and turn a knob to light the gas to start cooking. While the chores may differ, it is nevertheless necessary for the home maker to organise the household into a certain routine in which the essential chores fall into a systematic pattern.

Organising the household entails not only systematising different chores but also ensuring the cooperation of all family members and the domestic help, if any. By seeking the participation of the whole family there would be a joint effort towards the common goal of having a happy home in which all members find contentment and peace of mind.

The household should be organised in a flexible way so that all exigencies are taken care of. For example, a fixed cleaning schedule should not be placed above the needs of a family member who may be unwell and hence in need of extra sleep to make up for a disturbed night. Organisation should not be equated with rigidity and inflexibility.

Management of the household depends upon the type of house you own, the time you have and the will to carry out the affairs efficiently.

Types of Houses

Ever since civilization began, human beings have tried to live in a sheltered abode. From the ancient to the modern times man has striven to make his abode into a place of shelter, comfort and beauty. Starting from the cave paintings of Ajanta-Ellora to the fabulous gem studded palaces of royalty, there has been a constant endeavour for man to live amidst beautiful surroundings. Even villagers living in mud-huts decorate their walls with paintings so that they look attractive.

Today one lives either in a bungalow or increasingly, in a flat or apartment in a high rise building. Fortune smiles only on a few lucky ones who live in farm houses, independent houses, castles and palaces. For the general public one can at best aspire to own an apartment, hopefully a spacious one.

The type of house required differs from person to person and on one's circumstances as well as one's economic status. A family which is growing requires more space, whereas a single person or an elderly couple would find it burdensome to maintain a huge apartment or even a bungalow.

Therefore, in choosing a house or flat, individual's requirements, budget constraints, and the place or city in which one is living, plays a critical role in the selection of a flat or apartment.

What Our Home Says About Us

Interiors—we make them, and they make us. They shape our spirit, pushing us towards comfort or austerity.

Anyone who's ever trailed from door to door in the most anonymous block of flats will have noted the very individual smell that comes from each human burrow.

A home doesn't invariably reveal someone's job, though actors and artists often have rather self-conscious interiors (sometimes self-consciously conventional) as if they're on display, even to themselves; and pop and football stars' homes are instantly recognisable—awards glinting in gilt-encrusted settings which display money earned beyond their owners' wildest dreams.

Our interiors say a lot about the way we see the world. Researchers believe people are oriented in one of three ways: visually, audially, or kinetically (which means feelingly).

A "visual" focuses his or her room very clearly round an object, the fire-place, perhaps, or the TV; an "audial" has radios or hi-fi in most rooms, displays objects as "talking points" and creates areas for easy communication. "Kinetics", on the other hand, spread themselves and their belongings over comfortable sofas and soft carpets.

Home, as the saying goes, is where the heart is. And it's certainly where most of our treasures are kept—and most of our dreams, too. For, in the creation of our modest palaces, most of us are in a way, trying to fulfil a dream. Most of us tread softly when first we enter a home, exclaiming pleasantly over this light or that mirror, however banal or ugly it may seem in truth. We do this because we know how vulnerable the owner is—how their house is a subtle blend of what they are and what they hope to be, and they are offering this to us if only we have eyes to see.

Utilising space effectively

In modern life two things are at premium—time and space, hence both must be used effectively so that there is no wastage. The best way to utilise space effectively is to follow the motto—"a place for everything and everything in its place". In some duplex flats or double-storeyed houses, the space below the stairs can be effectively utilised for storage. The top of cupboards can be used for storing empty suitcases, while beds could have drawers in which linen or mattresses can be placed. In a small flat it is best to keep things to a minimum so that there is no clutter. Storage units and cupboards should be neatly lined with newspaper, brown paper or coloured paper and crockery, clothing, books arranged neatly so that essentials are within one's reach.

If the house is a shelter consisting of walls, floors, doors, windows and a roof under which human beings live, a home is a house in which a family or even an individual enjoys happiness, privacy, good health, ease and comfort. It is also a place where one entertains, has social interaction and indulges in one's hobbies. A home is one's sanctum sanctorum where one can relax, meditate and pray. If one builds one's own house then that becomes, in our country, a life time investment unlike in the west where people buy and sell houses frequently. Those who purchase their own apartment or buy a readymade house have to accept, for the greater part, the built-in infrastructure. Those who build their own house or those who acquire flats/houses in a modular state can put in fittings according to their taste and requirement such as the bathroom and kitchen tiling, the placement of storage cupboards and lofts, electrical fittings and so on. If one is fortunate enough to build one's own house, then with the help of an architect it could be designed to suit the needs of the family as well as to take full advantage of Nature in the sense that the sun, the wind, the aspect and the view are taken into consideration during construction. If it is bright, cheerful and airy, it would certainly guarantee that the owners would enjoy living in it. Perhaps the single most important element in the design of a small compact house or an apartment is the feeling of openness and space and the efficient use of this space. Proper orientation or the setting or facing of the plan of a building ensures that the inhabitants enjoy to the utmost whatever is good and avoid whatever is bad in respect of comfort and the normal elements such as the sun, wind, rain, topography and outlook and at the same time it provides a convenient access to both street and backyard.

While in most western countries, an aspect which gives the maximum sunshine is preferred as in these latitudes the sun never goes overhead, being always to the south of the zenith. The requirement in India and other tropical countries is exactly the opposite. The sun's heat in tropical countries must be kept to a minimum, particularly in summer when its rays are vertically overhead. The purpose of proper orientation is that the house or flat must be protected from the sun's direct rays during the day and from indirect heat during the night. The sun's action in causing heat is mostly direct by day but by night it is entirely indirect since the stone, brick or tiles of which the walls are made, absorb the sun's heat by day and radiate this heat at night. While doing so, the air in contact with them is heated, which is the real cause of discomfort during night. Thus, proper orientation must ensure that the house is protected both from the sun's direct heat by day and the indirect one at night.

The total heat absorbed depends on two factors, namely the intensity of the heat and its duration. The main aim of proper orientation is to admit the required amount of sunshine into the house in the morning when it is very pleasant and the intensity of its heat is less, and to minimise its duration in the afternoon and evening when its rays are again likely to enter the house. While the sun's rays are potent enough to kill germs, severe heat is not necessary for this purpose. The morning sun is satisfactory for this purpose so it is necessary that a certain amount of sun enters the house but it should be "shut out" when it becomes warmer. Merely closing down the windows for this purpose is not practical because the walls will still become heated and then radiation will make the rooms on that side quite uncomfortable. Hence, the building must be faced in such a way that the sun's rays will be effectively excluded without closing the windows in the late hours of the morning, especially in summer. If a certain amount of sunlight is allowed to penetrate into the house in the early morning, it is bound to do so also for a few hours in the late evening on the opposite side as well. Deep verandahs or sunshades in the south and the west would effectually exclude these strong evening rays.

The direction of the prevailing wind, especially in summer is between the west and the south but the exact angle depends on a number of local influences. Therefore, bedrooms, for example which are occupied at night must be located in its direction.

While a number of varying factors affect the consideration of planning a domestic building, no hard and fast rules can be laid down as no two sites would have identical conditions nor would individual requirements and idiosyncrasies be the same. Nevertheless certain features are common in the planning of buildings of all categories intended for use as residential accommodation. Among these are the above mentioned—aspect, privacy, grouping, spaciousness, sanitation, flexibility, circulation, practical considerations and furniture requirements. The shape of the plan is governed by the configuration of the building plot and its nature whether compact and closed or extended and open, and influenced by the local climatic factors. Where the climate is very cold, such as in Shimla, the plan should be closed and compact. Similarly, in the plains where it is very hot such as in Allahabad, the extreme heat in summer makes it mandatory to design a house with one or two central lofty apartments, ventilated and lighted by means of skylights below the ceiling. On the sea coast such as Bombay or Madras, moisture rather than heat affects comfort. The object here is to expose as much of the area of the house to outside air so that a lot of breeze is able to come into the rooms. Hence, an open extended plan shaped like the letters L, E, U or H with large windows on the outside walls is appropriate for the climate.

Aspect refers to the arrangement of the doors and windows on the outside walls of the dwelling so that the gifts of Nature in terms of the sun, air, and view are incorporated in the planning. Aspect not only provides comfort but is necessary from the hygienic point of view as well. The value of the sun's rays in destroying germs and comfort cannot be overemphasized. By careful positioning of the windows it is possible to admit the sun's rays into any room as desired. A kitchen should have an eastern aspect so that the morning sun streams in and that it would be cool in the latter part of the day. The bedrooms should have a south-east or south-west aspect, while the drawing room a north-east or south-east one.

Privacy is essential in a house and is of two types:

1. Screening of the interior of any one room from the other rooms in the house and also from the main entrance.
2. The privacy of the whole house from the street.

Privacy is of great importance and is especially important for bedrooms, bathrooms and the kitchen. As far as possible, every room except perhaps the drawing room shall have an independent access to it. The skill of the architect is called for while planning these aspects of any house or flat.

Grouping refers to the placement of rooms in relation to each other. For example, the kitchen should be close to the dining room but away from the main living room so that the smoke and smells from the kitchen do not bother those in the living area. Similarly the toilets should be accessible from the bedrooms.

Spaciousness refers to the effect produced by making the best of small proportions of rooms, by deriving the maximum benefit from the minimum dimensions of the room. Alternately maximum benefit should be derived from the minimum dimension of a room to give it a feeling of being roomy. This again requires a great deal of skill on the part of the architect as a room whose walls are disproportionately high, looks much smaller than what it actually is. Similarly, if the length of a room exceeds its width, it looks cramped. A square room looks smaller than an oblong one and in terms of utility this is also true. Space should be well utilised for cupboards, such as under the staircase, below the windows and so on.

Furniture requirements for different rooms must be kept in mind. For example, the positioning of the bed is very important in a bedroom and provision must be made for it. It is necessary to exercise forethought and imagination so that there is provision in every room for the placement of essential furniture.

Sanitation is of primary importance in a dwelling for the health of its inhabitants. The importance of light and suitable sanitation arrangements must be built into the plan. Dust is another great enemy of human health as it causes the spread of many diseases. No mouldings or even skirtings and cornices should be allowed in the inner surfaces of walls as dirt and dust accumulate in them. Ledges, nooks, crevices and all other spaces in which dust can settle should be avoided. All edges and corners and angles made by junctions of walls with floors and ceilings should be rounded.

Ventilation is a prerequisite for any room as it means that the stale air will exit from the rooms and also the maintenance of a movement of air within the house. Movement or the lack of movement of air in a house or the lack of it can lead to a feeling of well-being or discomfort. Lack of movement of air, especially in a tropical country leads to the increase in temperature and humidity which in turn leads to lack of evaporation from the body surface and the subsequent accumulation of heat. For cross ventilation, one window situated in the centre of an outer wall is insufficient. It is, therefore, necessary to have another window or windows in the opposite wall. The so-called "stuffiness" in a crowded room is caused not only by the partial exhaustion of oxygen and the presence of an undue amount of carbonic gas in it, but more by the fact that there are human exhalations in it which are warm, and contain water vapour. Also germs and odours emanating from these exhalations add to the stuffiness in the atmosphere. The purpose of ventilation, therefore, is:

a) to give a sensation of comfortable coolness to the body
b) freedom from bad odours
c) reduction of humidity, and
d) proper supply of oxygen.

A house is arranged into various rooms for the comfort of its inhabitants and each room is required for a different purpose. The size of a house, apartment or duplex apartment may vary but if possible there should be different rooms so that family members and guests can come together and stay in comfort.

Time Management

For a household to function smoothly, time management is as valuable at home as it is in an office. Effective time management ensures that there is no pressure to hurry and perform tasks at breakneck speed, as in household chores the old adage, "haste makes waste" is true. If one tries to cook too fast, put the milk to boil on high heat or if one washes or takes out dishes in a hurry, there is a danger of spilling or breaking things. Hence, allowing reasonable amount of time for different chores, one can always work backwards. For example, if it takes an hour to get the children ready for school with their breakfast and lunch boxes, and if they have to leave the house at 7 a.m., it is best to start at 6 a.m. so that unnecessary hurry is avoided. Working against the pressure of time increases anxiety and gives rise to tension.

The full-time housewife is the mistress of her time, but for those who are working, the time would have to be divided into pre-office and post-office segments, with household chores being divided accordingly. The full-time housewife would divide her day with different chores being performed at different times. For example, early morning chores such as giving the children their breakfast and tiffin and sending them to school, organising her husband's breakfast and packed lunch and supervising the work of the domestic help.

The latter part of the day would include cooking lunch, daily shopping and arranging social calls. Once the children return from school, they would have their lunch, and then study. The evening would revolve around the preparation of dinner, the return of the husband from office and of older children from college. The arrival of guests would necessitate extra preparations according to the situation.

The housewife has the innate advantage of being able to organise her schedule according to her needs, thus giving her great flexibility of movement. In the afternoon a visit to the beauty parlour, a hobby lesson or a visit to the market are all within her ambit.

Having chalked out her schedule for the day, there is still a lot that can be done when there are a few minutes to spare.

The following can be done in 5 minutes:

a) an appointment made with a doctor, lawyer or dentist
b) a list of guests can be made for a party
c) indoor plants can be watered
d) a button can be sewed
e) nails can be filed.

The following can be done in 10 minutes:
a) some exercises
b) washing a few clothes or dishes

c) tidying the top of the desk
d) dusting
e) writing out short notes, letters or birthday cards.

One can do the following in 30 minutes:

a) one can go through the newspaper or magazines
b) polish silver or brass
c) do some ironing
d) make phone calls
e) work on some craft project or arrange flowers.

Organising Household Chores

Household chores are of three or four types and can be divided into those that are compulsory and those that are optional, those that must be done daily and others which are weekly or monthly.

Chores for the Day

These include cleaning the house, dusting, bed making, clothes washing, dish washing and cooking.

In western countries where houses are thermetically sealed to keep out the cold, there is less dust, fewer guests and frequently no children. Hence, it is possible to vacuum the house once a week and cook in bulk once every second or third day. However, if a similar schedule were to be adopted in India, the end result would be disastrous! Due to the heat and frequent electricity failure, eating food that has been cooked and kept for two or three days in the 'fridge' is fraught with risk. Moreover, the houses are open hence there is a considerable amount of dust and dirt which comes as children, guests and domestic help come in and out of the house. Hence, in India it is essential to cook and clean on a daily basis.

Most Indian families have four meals per day, in addition to the tiffin for school children and office goers. Apart from this, snacks must be offered along with a beverage to visitors who drop in. Thus, cooking, cleaning and dishwashing have to be done on a daily basis, if not several times a day.

The heat and humidity make the stacking of clothes, so that they can be washed in one lot in the washing machine, an unhygienic proposition in the Indian climate. Hence, clothes washing is, also, necessarily a daily chore irrespective of whether one washes by hand or in a machine. Thus, there is really no short-cut to the drudgery of performing certain chores on a daily basis. If one looks upon these tasks in a positive way it becomes easier as it is indeed a pleasure to live in a clean house, wear freshly washed clothes and eat well-cooked meals on sparkling dishes.

Some amount of shopping as for milk, bread and fresh vegetables and fruit is also a daily feature of an Indian household.

Weekly Chores

Certain household chores can be done on a weekly basis such as shopping for meat, fish, eggs, chicken as well as fruits and vegetables. Fruits and vegetables must be stored carefully in the 'fridge' as they are perishable products. For example, bananas turn black if kept in the 'fridge'.

The bed linen and table linen must be changed once a week, along with hand towels and bath towels. In case there are house guests, they must be given fresh sheets and towels.

Bedspreads can be changed once in two weeks.

Monthly Chores

These would include grocery shopping and "rations" such as rice, wheat, dals or pulses, flour, tea, sugar and edible oil as well as spices and detergents. Every housewife would have a rough idea of the family's monthly consumption and would purchase according to the requirement with a little extra for guests and visitors.

Another important monthly chore is the payment of bills and payment to the domestic help. Bills and salaries should be paid promptly and one can have a diary or account book in which accounts are maintained on a daily, weekly and monthly basis.

Some cleaning chores can be done on a monthly basis, such as the cleaning of doors and windows. The mattresses and pillows can also be put in the sun once a month.

Maintaining the Household Records

While people in other parts of the world may be moving towards a paperless society, we in India cannot afford to adopt a casual attitude towards paper as we live in a "paper raj". Electricity, water and telephone bills along with their receipts, house tax, municipal tax, income tax and children's school fee receipts must be kept with the utmost care. There are so many instances of double billing and claims of "non-receipt of payment", that it is vitally important for all bills and their receipts to be kept carefully for many years as a measure of both caution and necessity.

Photocopies of important documents can be made and kept in another place such as in a safe deposit vault or in the work place so that they are not destroyed in the event of a fire or flood.

Bills, taxes, insurance policies, children's school records and a separate medical file for each member of the family should be kept in well marked and easily accessible plastic folders.

A list should be made of the last date for the payment of telephone, electricity, water, credit card and club bills and payment should be made before the last date so that one can avail of the possible rebate given for early payment.

Household insurance and car insurance policies should be kept in separate files so that payment for renewal can be made prior to the expiry date.

Important papers can be thrown away only after a suitable period has elapsed and when one is sure that they are no longer relevant. All important papers have to be scanned periodically so that unnecessary clutter is not created.

■■

CHAPTER-2

Cleaning the House and its Security

Cleaning the house is a daily chore and due to the high levels of dust, dirt and pollution in our environment it is compulsory to conduct at least once a day, some 'mopping up' operation. Unlike in the western countries where houses are thermatically sealed to keep out the cold, houses in India are open to cope with the vagaries of nature. Therefore, it is not enough to vacuum the house once or twice a week as is common in the west. Also, homes in India have much more traffic in terms of visitors, family members, domestic help, and others who come in and out of the house. Thus cleaning the house is a daily essential and all members of the house must contribute towards this end. Every homemaker has a standard of cleanliness for the home and if these standards are not adhered to and if the house is disordered or dirty, the housewife feels uncomfortable .

Self Help

The pressure of cooking meals, washing clothes, caring for the children, working at home or outside makes it difficult for the housewife to keep the house clean on her own. Frequent light cleaning is the most economical. The homemaker with a schedule and sound methods is better equipped, not only to do the task at hand, but also to teach and guide her assistants whether they are members of the family or paid employees. The main object is to make the job easier and less tiresome by taking a few practical steps.

a) Daily cleaning consists chiefly of sweeping, swabbing and dusting the rooms. In the bedroom, beds must be made and covered with a bed cover.

b) Rooms should be dusted after sweeping but before swabbing so that the consequent dust is mopped up by a wet cloth and is not allowed to circulate and pollute the air.

c) Rugs should be brushed with a carpet brush and so should the upholstery.

d) Weekly cleaning follows the same general procedure but must be done thoroughly. Pictures, mirrors, light bulbs and light fixtures, closet floors, backs of furniture and window shades are dusted.

e) Wherever there is too much dust it is advisable to wipe with a damp cloth.

f) Every other week upholstered furniture may be cleaned with a vacuum cleaner.

g) Mattresses may be put in the sun and turned side for side one week and end to end the next.

h) Light bulbs, enclosing globes and shades in a few rooms should be cleaned each week so that all are included once a month.

i) Draperies and curtains may be washed or dry-cleaned as and when required.

j) Furniture should be polished from time to time.

k) Rugs and carpets have to be rolled so that the floor beneath can be wiped.

l) In case one has a lawn, sunning a carpet and then pulling it along the grass effectively removes a lot of dust and dirt and prevents the carpet from getting damaged as it may through improper vacuuming and dry cleaning.

Domestic Help

India is perhaps one of the few countries in the world where the housewife has the option of keeping servants. Domestic help makes the task of the homemaker easier. However, one should keep the following points in mind:

a) Assign specified tasks to your domestic help, e.g. sweeping, washing.

b) Explain to him/her where you help your clearing utensils.

c) Specify the days of the week when special cleaning needs to be done, e.g. cleaning the carpets, sunning the mattress, etc.

d) If you have more than one servant, assign separate tasks to each of them to avoid confusion and ensure efficiency.

e) You can also explain to them your cleaning schedule.

The situation of servants, however, varies throughout the country, e.g. in Bombay part-time help is more common. Whereas in Delhi, you have the option of both. Hence, depending on the situation, you can decide whether you would like to have all full-time servants or a combination of full-time and part-time or only part-time servants. Many newly married couples, where both the spouses are working, prefer the option of part-time servants as this enables them to lock the house before going off to work.

Types of Cleaning Tools

Brooms

A good broom is essential for cleaning the house. It may be made of vegetable fibres or a harder broom with sticks can be used for washing verandahs, kitchen and the extended portion of the house.

Brushes

There are many types of domestic brushes ranging from a hard bristled carpet brush to a bottle brush, toilet brush, shoe brush, clothes brush, bath tub brush.

Mops

Mops should be washed in suds as often as necessary to keep them clean and then rinsed and dried in the sun. Dry mops also require washing but they are not so frequently used in India as wooden parquet floors are rarely used.

Duster clothes and sponges

Dusters may be made from old clothing, towels, or household fabrics. Pieces of fine, soft wool make the most satisfactory dusting cloth or linen. Chamois is excellent for washing windows because it cleans and polishes at the same time. It is made of sheep skin and is oil tanned. The quality of a chamois can be judged by its elasticity. Sponges are better than cloth for washing walls, tiles and stone surfaces. Sponges and steel wool sponges are often used for cleaning utensils. Damp and crushed newspapers are a good way of cleaning glass surfaces without scratching them.

Dustpans and pails

Dustpans with long handles eliminate stooping. However, since most of the sweeping in houses is done by a domestic servant by squatting, a smaller dustpan can also be used. A separate pail made of either steel or plastic should be kept for wiping the floors.

Vacuum cleaners

A vacuum cleaner is one of the most useful household tools because it removes dust and

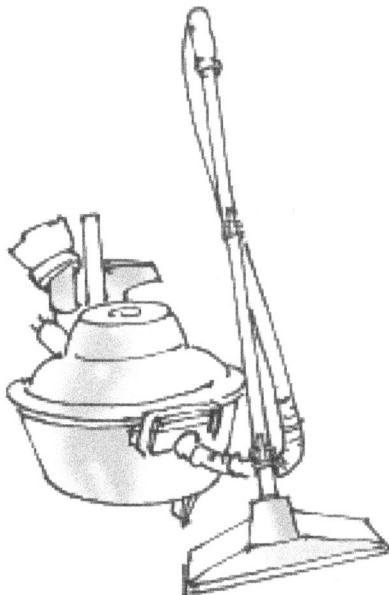

litter effectively. Suction sweeping and agitation are employed in the different types of vacuum

cleaners to remove dust. Vacuum cleaners are particularly useful on areas which are carpeted.

Cleaning supplies

Water, particularly warm water is a good cleaning agent. Although it loosens dirt, it should be used sparingly and wiped off quickly. It should never be allowed to stand on wall, floor or furniture, nor should it be allowed to soak into seams and cracks.

Detergents

Some synthetic detergents are superior to soap for washing dishes and clothes.

Polishes

Waxes and metal polishes protect the floor, furniture and metals respectively. They not only give a shine but also offer protection against insects. Since wooden floors cannot be swabbed with soap and water, it must be waxed. Light scratches on wooden furniture and wooden floor can also be eliminated by waxing and polishing.

Maintaining the Walls

Get your house painted at least once in two years.

Sometimes washing walls is also a feasible option. You will need:

a) Sturdy ladder
b) Detergent mix
c) Clean water
d) 2 buckets.

Always remember to start at the top as this avoids permanent staining due to the detergent. First wipe the wall with a washing sponge, then rinse out the dirt into an empty bucket. Now restart the process by dipping your sponge into the cleaning solution. Avoid using coloured sponges as this may leave stains. Now wipe the walls dry with terry cloth towels

However, weekly cleaning of ceiling is also a must. Always start high up. You will need a duster and a stepladder.

Another handy hint is to apply a thin coat of laundry starch after washing the walls. This will make your task easier the next time around.

Maintaining the Floors

a) Never scrub wooden floors with water. Dry mopping and sweeping is sufficient for a routine cleaning.

b) Never use an oiled dust mop on a waxed floor.

c) Clean varnished floors with a long handled brush and a dust mop.

d) Waxed floors—to remove excess polish, use a special floor cleaner and a scotch brite pad. Don't forget to wear gloves. For a regular cleaning, use cheesecloth and one can renew finish with liquid wax.

e) Ordinary mosaic flooring or tiled flooring is cleaned most effectively with a sweeping mop and a floor cleaner e.g. Domex, Phenyl, etc.

f) To avoid scratching your flooring while shifting furniture, either lift the furniture or slip old socks over the legs of the table before sliding it.

Maintaining Tiles

a) Tiles in the bathroom should be washed at least once in two days with a sponge and detergent soap.

b) Ceramic tiles on walls or floors should also be cleaned with the help of a household cleaner and a sponge/mop.

c) To make ceramic tiles look fresh, brush white shoe polish into the cracks around the tiles (using an old toothbrush). Wipe off the polish streaks with a damp cloth.

Cleaning Carpets

Use a carpet sweeper to remove dirt daily.

Do not attempt to shake your carpets violently.

Do not varnish the floor under the carpets as the dirt that seeps through ruins the varnish.

To make your sweeping more efficient drop some moist newspaper strips before sweeping.

While vacuuming your carpet remember to move your vacuum in the direction of the pile. Work in overlapping parallel strokes paying special attention to areas in front of furniture pieces.

For shampooing carpets, you will need an aerosol spray foam. First vacuum your carpet thoroughly then apply an even layer of foam over the surface of the carpet. Now let the foam dry thoroughly then vacuum the carpet at top suction. Or alternatively, you could also use any detergent that you use for washing woollen clothes. To drain out the water from the carpet, use a long wooden stick with rubber attachment. Allow the carpet to dry thoroughly before placing back in the room.

To store away carpets, first sun them for at least two-three days, clean them thoroughly. Spread dried *neem* leaves all along the surface. Roll tightly and wrap in brown paper.

Lay carpets only on level surfaces.

Spray the underlay with insecticide at regular intervals.

Turn the carpets around at frequent intervals to distribute the weight of the furniture.

Do not use hard brushes on carpets as the pile gets disturbed.

Do not drag heavy furniture over carpets. Also move heavy furniture around frequently to avoid crushing a carpet.

Protect carpets from strong sunlight.

Another effective way of shampooing your carpet is to use the foam collected from reetha nuts. Apply the foam and start cleaning the carpet from one end. Rub the lather in a circular motion.

You could add 1 teaspoonful of vinegar to the shampoo to yield better results.

Tips for removing carpet stains:

a) Always work inwards from the edge of the stain.
b) Apply only small amounts of cleaning agent at a time.
c) Never overwet the pile carpet.
d) Rinse the treated area with clean water.

Removing Spots from Rugs

Food Stains: Use ordinary washing methods. For radical procedure, add 3 tablespoonfuls ammonia to 2 gallons of suds.

Oil Stains: (from fibre rugs). Apply cleaning fluid periodically until stain is removed from rug permanently.

Ink Stains: Flush out stain with water, blot with soft, dry cloth. Or apply fresh milk as quickly after the accident as possible. Cover with cornstarch and remove, and then apply solution of mild soap and water. If stain persists, apply paste of milk and cornmeal and allow to remain overnight. If stain still persists, loosen with ink eradicator No.1 solution, then sponge with oxalic acid, and wash with water to which 3 drops of ammonia have been added, wash with clear water.

Paint: Apply turpentine, soap and water. If paint has hardened, soften with paint remover, scrape, and then apply turpentine. Don't use liquid paint remover if stain is wet.

Argyrol: Dissolve 2 tablets dichloride of mercury in 1 ounce water. Apply with dropper till stain disappears. Remove solution. Rinse dry.

Iodine: 1 ounce hyposulphite in 3 ounces water. Add 1/2 ounce ammonia; apply with dropper till stain disappears.

Rust Stains: Apply a mild solution of oxalic acid and rinse immediately.

Shoe Polish: Use dry-cleaning fluid, then wash with solution of ammonia, soap and water.

Cleaning Curtains/Blinds

Curtains

You can dry-clean your curtains once in 6 months.

However, you can wash the lighter curtains at home once in 2 months either in a washing machine or with the help of a detergent.

Remember to wax the curtain rods every time you wash your curtains.

If a freshly washed curtain does not hang well, send it for a steam press to the drycleaner.

Blinds

a) Venetian blinds - to clean use a feather duster. However, for a special clean up take them down and wash in a detergent.

b) Holland blinds - use the dusting attachment for your vacuum cleaner or take down and scrub with detergent.

c) Plastic blinds - should be washed in detergent and hung to drip dry.

Maintaining Upholstery

Fine fabrics and pale coloured upholstery should be given to the dry cleaner.

If cleaning at home make sure you use the upholstery shampoo according to the instructions.

Brush upholstery once a week with a carpet brush.

Polishing Silver

Maintaining silver articles around the house is a demanding task as sulphur compounds in the air cause it to tarnish easily. To keep your silverware shining:

Electrolysis: This process is an effective way to remove tarnish. Fill an aluminium vessel with hot water (before using the vessel boil it in a weak vinegar solution). To the hot water, add 1 tsp. of salt, and 1 tsp. of baking powder for each quart of water. Bring the water to boil and drop in the pieces of silver. In a few seconds, the silver will be bright. Now wash in soap water. Rinse and wipe dry with a soft cloth.

Silver polishes are equally efficient. Remember to follow the instructions on the bottle.

While washing silverware, separate cutlery and tableware to avoid scratches. Soak in warm soapy water. Rub well and rinse with hot water. Now lay them on a clean towel to dry.

To remove egg stains from your silverware, sprinkle salt on it and then rub with a wet cloth.

Lacquer your ornamental silver to prevent tarnishing.

Wash oxidised silver in lukewarm water and soap at frequent intervals.

Furniture

Marks on furniture
Scratch marks

Fine scratches can be disguised by rubbing with half a Brazil nut kernel. The oil from the nut will darken the scratch so it tones with the surrounding surface.

Alternatively, dip a piece of flannel in linseed oil, then lay it over the scratch and press it down firmly. Leave it for three hours, remove the cloth and rub in a good wax polish, again leaving it for a few hours before dusting off.

Deep scratches can be filled with plastic wood or wood stopping in a suitable colour, applied with an orange stick.

Spilled perfume, hair spray or nail varnish

Don't try to wipe off the spilled liquid, because this simply makes the mark worse. Leave it to dry before tackling the problem.

If the damage is slight and only the top layer of polish has been affected, try rubbing it lightly with 9/0 grade (very fine) sand paper. Rub uniformly over the entire surface, working in the direction of the grain. This will gradually remove a thin film of polish together with the marks.

Once the marks have disappeared you can rub the surface with metal polish applied with a damp cloth, to revive the gloss. Then buff up with a clean duster.

Heat marks and water marks

On a varnished surface you may find that the marks will disappear if you rub them with metal polish. Follow this up with brown shoe polish applied sparingly with a soft cloth, and buff up well.

On polished furniture you can rub the marks with a cloth which has been moistened with a mixture of linseed oil and turpentine. You can make this yourself by adding 1/4 pint of turpentine to 1 pint of linseed oil (the boiled variety). Mix well, rub the mixture into the affected areas, leave overnight then polish. Keep the mixture in a bottle for future use.

Cleaning up teak

To cure marks from sticky fingers, hot dishes and cosmetics, apply white spirit (turps substitute) on a lint-free cloth, then rub with a very fine grade (000) wire wool, rubbing along the direction of the grain only (if you go across the grain you will scratch the surface). After this wipe over the surface with a cloth moistened with white spirit, then dry off with a dry cloth. Finish off by applying teak oil in the normal way.

Upholstered furniture

Non-grease marks should be sponged with a soft cloth wrung out in cool water. Remove grease marks with a spirit dry-cleaning solvent such as carbon tetrachloride, applied with a soft clean cloth.

Alternatively, the odd grease marks can be treated with French chalk or fuller's earth. Leave overnight to absorb the grease and then brush off the following morning. If this hasn't removed the mark, repeat the process several times. If the mark is on the back of the furniture and the powder does not stay put, mix it with a little carbon tetrachloride to form a thick paste and spread this over the stain.

On wool, tapestry and velveteen to remove light surface dirt, first vacuum the furniture thoroughly with a shaped cleaning nozzle. Then use a soft, clean cloth moistened with cleaning fluid, such as carbon tetrachloride, and rub lightly over the upholstery. Alternatively, wring out a cloth tightly in mild detergent suds and rub over the surface. Dry foam shampoo cleaners applied with a large-pored sponge are also suitable for these materials—and for Dralon flat-woven and Dralon velvet upholstery. Velvet, brocatelle, silk and non-fast coloured fabrics should be professionally cleaned. Vinyl upholstery should be washed with a cloth wrung out in mild soapless detergent or soapflakes. Scrub heavy vinyl but never use chemicals, soda, strong soap powders or abrasives. To remove ballpoint ink stains, sponge with a cloth moistened with methylated spirit and then rinse well. Another method is to rub the stain with a cloth dipped in neat liquid detergent.

Hide furniture needs dusting and occasionally a rub with liquid silicone polish. To treat soiled hide, clean it with a cloth dipped in a solution of half vinegar and half-warm water. Leave to dry then rub with linseed oil. Leave for twenty-four hours then rub off any remaining oil and polish with white silicone cream.

Wooden furniture is usually finished with varnish lacquer or shellac and rubbed to a high polish. To dust, use a clean dry hemmed duster and give each piece an extra rub to keep it shining. Always use coasters when serving drinks or heat-resistant pads to take your dishes. Wipe up spills immediately and then rub with the palm of your hand or a cloth moistened with oil polish.

For old stains, use powdered pumice mixed to a paste with linseed oil. Rub lightly in the direction of the grain. Wipe with a cloth soaked in plain linseed oil.

Deep-seated stains should be treated professionally.

Candlewax must be scraped off with a stiff card or your fingernail. Wash with warm soapsuds.

Grease spots should be wiped with a cloth moistened with cleaning fluid and then polished. For ink spills, blot it up quickly and apply a damp cloth to the spot, pressing firmly. Continue blotting with a dampened cloth using a clean portion every time. Don't rub the ink in.

Wipe off fresh paint blotches with a cloth dipped in turpentine polish.

Soften old spots with linseed oil. Soak for a while. Scrape away softened paint and use pumice stone treatment for remaining traces of polish.

A well-waxed surface is a safeguard against watermarks.

Bamboo or cane furniture should be dusted with a damp cloth to prevent the drying out or splitting of this type of furniture.

Leather upholstered furniture should be dry dusted. To prevent leather from cracking, rub it occasionally with castor oil on dark surfaces and white Vaseline on light surfaces. Wipe out all traces of oil thoroughly. Upholstered furniture should be kept clean with a good stiff brush.

Appliances

Wash your pressure cooker after each use, but do not immerse the cover in water to avoid clogging the vents. Wipe the cover with a soapy cloth, and rinse with a damp one. Clean openings and draw a string through them. Carefully wash the gasket. Reversing the gasket sometimes helps if steam tends to escape from the cooker.

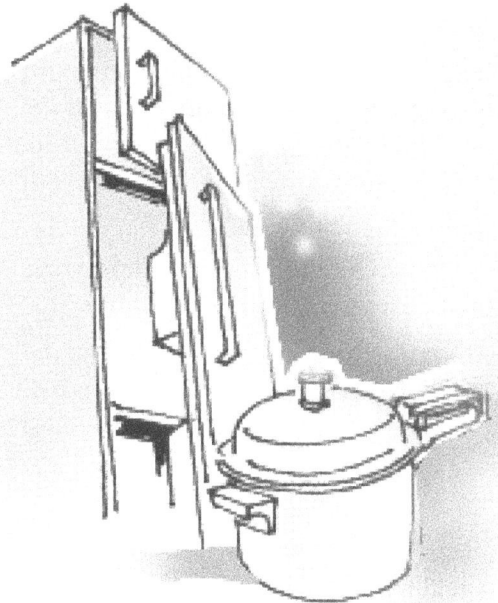

Refrigerators should be defrosted before the frost is more than an inch thick. Clean out the interior. Remove all the food from the shelves.

Clean and wipe all surfaces. Clean gasket and accessories with soap and water. Rinse and wipe dry. Clean the outside of a refrigerator at least once a month.

Let hot dishes partially cool before refrigerating them.

Keep the refrigerator full. A half-empty appliance uses more energy because air is harder to keep cold than chilled food.

Cover dishes with moisture and vapour proof wraps to prevent frost from forming and liquid from evaporating. This will help retain flavour too.

Electric bulbs should be dusted regularly and washed once a month to get full lighting value. Shades and glass fixtures should be given the same treatment.

Electric wires should be replaced or repaired if frazzled or worn out to ensure against short circuits and shock.

Before connecting or disconnecting a cord turn off the switch. If the appliance itself is controlled by a switch, switch it off before connecting or disconnecting it to prevent sparking and wearing away of contacts.

Jerking plugs out may damage copper wires inside or the prongs of the plug.

Never wrap cord around an iron or a heater while still warm. Store cords loosely in a box or drawer or hang them coiled over a round peg.

Electric fans. Oil your fan about once a year. To clean an electric fan, first disconnect it. Wipe blades and motor casing with a damp cloth. If the casing is very dirty, use a cloth wrung out of soap suds taking care not to let any moisture permeate the casing. Rinse and dry. When storing your fan, cover it completely with paper or a cloth.

Electric iron. Always disconnect the iron as soon as you've finished your work and allow it to cool. If the bottom has become stained with starch, wipe it with a cloth wrung out of hot soap suds. Never scrape with a knife. Avoid using the iron over zippers, hooks or buttons as it might scratch the plating. About once a month, rub the bottom with paraffin or beeswax, carefully wiping out surplus with a piece of cloth or paper. This keeps the iron slick and prevents starch stains. Replace worn cords promptly. When ironing don't press too hard.

Stoves. Wipe food spills immediately, while the stove is still warm.

Cleaning Light Fixtures

a) Wipe light fixtures with a damp cloth at least once a month. However, make sure you shut the mains off.

b) To clean chandeliers spray with glass cleaner till the dirt starts dripping. Now wipe off with a soft cloth. However, switch off the mains.

c) Always remove bulbs from the fixtures before cleaning.

d) To clean tubelights use a cloth dipped in detergent. Then wipe off with a soft dry cloth.

Handling Domestic Garbage

Provide waste paper baskets in every room to take care of everyday garbage.

These waste paper baskets should be cleaned out everyday.

Wash these baskets once a week to keep them clean.

One big bin should be provided where the garbage of the house should be thrown. Line this bin with special garbage bags to facilitate cleaning. This bin should also be cleaned everyday, and washed with Dettol once a month.

On old stains try vinegar and rinse carefully with water. Yellow stains that remain after treatment with detergent may require the use of bleach.

Should perspiration odour cling to washable materials after they have been laundered, soak them for an hour or more in warm water - 3 or 4 tbsp. of salt to a quart of water.

Always remove perspiration stains before ironing, as ironing a stain weakens the fabric.

Household Hints

Clear nail polish can often be substituted for glue. If a stamp or envelope won't stick, dab some on.

To catch drips from a tea or coffee pot, slit the centre of a paper coaster and slip it over the spout of a pot.

If hems of shirt or dress come undone, and you need to reattach them in a hurry, use cellophane tape.

To clean silver, try fine-pored, very soft sponges instead of cloth. They penetrate hard-to-reach crevices and rinse quickly.

To clean louvers on shutters and doors easily, use ice cream bar sticks wrapped in detergent saturated cloths.

Apply a little furniture wax to the insides of metal ashtrays. Ash won't cake on the bottoms and cleaning is much easier.

To wipe paint off hands, arms and face, try using cooking oil instead of the regular paint remover that often burns the skin.

Wash ice cube trays in hot, soapy water. This prevents them from sticking to the freezer compartment. Or, after defrosting the refrigerator and cleaning out the freezing compartment, place the trays on aluminium foil.

If a raw egg spills on the floor, avoid messy cleaning by covering it thickly with salt. Let it dry and sweep up.

To remove stubborn stains from stainless steel, use a scouring pad dipped in a mild solution of ammonia and water.

To brighten aluminium or other utensils, rub them with lemon peel, and then rinse with warm water.

Add a few drops of ammonia to finally rinse for sparkling glassware.

If pans get burnt, fill them with soapy water and boil the water for 10 minutes.

Cotton socks make a good applicator when you have to stain intricately carved pieces. First don a rubber glove, then pull on the socks.

Dip your fingers in the stain, then rub it on the work.

A clean cotton sock is also a handy dusting tool that works well on venetian blinds. Wear the socks on your hand and wipe the slats between the thumb and fingers. White tapes on the blinds that are slightly soiled or discoloured can be touched up with white liquid shoe polish.

Dust behind radiators or under appliances. You can easily make a dusting tool by slipping heavy cotton socks on a stick. Secure the socks with a rubber band, then spray it lightly with a dusting spray.

A stick can also become a handy tool for retrieving small parts that roll under the sofa or behind a cabinet.

Sealing a can of paint seems simple enough, but it can be difficult when paint collects in the rim groove. Use a thin nail to punch holes in the groove. The holes will allow the paint to drain back into the can and keep the groove clean.

When sealing the can, put a mark on the lid and a corresponding mark on the rim of the can. Always align these marks when resealing the can.

Finally, after pounding the lid in place, turn the can over and hold it upside down for a few seconds—be sure to support the lid with your hand. This upside-down posture will allow the paint to flow around the lid and form an airtight seal.

Keeping the garage floor clean: Sand is handy even if you don't have a pet—for whom a sand box can be useful before it learns toilet training. There is a better way to take care of nagging oil spills. Take a large metal lid or use an unused shallow pan. Put some sand in it and place it under the leaking engine. The sand will absorb the oil and can be changed anytime.

Problem of Household Pests

The problem of household pests such as ants, flies, silver fish, spiders, cockroaches and rats are particularly acute in a hot humid and crowded country like ours. Unless kept under control these pests cause a great deal of damage in the house. There are many professional pest control companies which come in and fumigate the house from time to time. However, many of these pests, particularly cockroaches have increasingly become resistant to these sprays. The key to keeping the pests away is to deny them food, water and a place in which they could find shelter. Food should be stored in tightly sealed glass or plastic containers (airtight). Crumbs and spills should be cleaned up immediately and counters and cabinets should be kept spotlessly clean. The sink area should be kept dry and garbage can should be cleaned out regularly and covered with a secure lid. Cracks and crevices in the walls should be filled in immediately. Electric bug zappers are not effective for bees, wasps and mosquitoes, however they do keep other flying insects away.

Black Ants: A black ant nests mostly on moist or decaying wood and can cause severe structural damage. The nest area has to be treated with a household formulation of chloropyrifos, diazinon, malathion or proposur.

Small ant or household ant: is attracted by sweet or greasy food. It can be traced by following the ants' path from the food supply to the nest. Apply dust or spray at points of entry into the house, beneath the refrigerator, cabinets, sinks and around table legs.

Termites or white ants: Call for professional treatment. To safeguard your precious books, spray with insecticide till eliminated.

Bed bugs: Spray every possible hiding space in an infested room. Bed bugs are commonly found in mattresses, box sprungs, floor and wall cracks, furniture and wall paper. They feed on human blood and appear flat and brown when empty and round and red when full. It is a nocturnal pest. Spray over the entire mattress paying particular attention to tufts, folds and seams. Let the bed remain unmade for one or two hours before sleeping in it. In treating cracks and crevices, spray until the liquid begins to run off. Spray walls upto several feet from the floor. A thoroughly administered single spray usually kills all insects present and leaves a film that protects for several months. If seen again after two weeks, the treatment must be repeated. Professional pest exterminators must be called in for badly infested houses.

Cockroaches: It is said that cockroaches will survive a nuclear holocaust. It is difficult to keep them away especially in multi-storeyed apartments as they creep in from flat to flat. They hide in moist, warm and dark areas and feed on food and garbage at night. Sprays and powder should be put around the stove and kitchen sink or underneath cupboards, behind refrigerators and in other hard to reach areas. Keeping *neem* leaves in the store cabinets and drawers is another method of keeping them at bay. Lining kitchen cabinets with newspaper or brown paper also reduces cockroaches.

Flour Moths: These flourish in flour, grain bud seed and pet food. Throw away all infested foods and store fresh supplies in tightly closed plastic or metal containers.

Silver Fish: These are found in cool, damp areas such as basements or cupboards. They feed on starches including glue and paste. They are nocturnal. Silverfish also attack clothes e.g., woollen sweaters, silk sarees, etc. One should treat cracks and openings around wall paper with a household formulation of diazinon, malathion or proposur. Another treatment is to remove all clothes and spray walls, doors and ceiling with 5 per cent DDT in oil or aerosol bombs containing pyrethium extract. In extreme cases professional help may be sought. To prevent damage by the silver fish, thorough cleaning and packing clothes in sealed packages containing flake naphthalene or para dichlorobenzene cedar lined chests may be dependable but not cedar lines closets. Rugs and upholstery should be brushed frequently in heat or cold. Seal off all cracks and openings. One could also hang in a muslin bag 1 lb of flake naphthalene or para dichlorobenzene to each 100 cubic feet.

Spiders: Spiders feed on insects. They are generally harmless except for the black widow and the brown recluse varieties. Spiders spin webs in corners and crevices that are unsightly and unsafe as spiders can cause skin allergies. Remove webs with dusting brush attachment. One could effectively keep them away by spraying kerosene, pyrethiun, and crushed white eggs.

Mosquitoes: The most common habitat for mosquitoes is stagnant water. Adult females feed on human and animal blood. Many of them transmit debilitating diseases, e.g., malaria, filaria, dengue fever, yellow fever and encephalitis. The most effective way of keeping them out is to have mosquito meshing on doors and windows. Alternatively mosquito sprays, repellants and electronic mosquito repellants can be used to prevent harmful mosquito bites.

Wasps or Hornets: These are found in attics, porch ceilings, roof-tops, trees and so on. There are many people who are allergic to their sting. Their outdoor nests should be treated with a commercial wasp and hornet spray. Mosquito meshing on doors and windows prevents their entry into the houses.

Houseflies: They thrive on food garbage and decaying organic matter such as manure or cut grass. Many diseases such as typhoid, jaundice can spread when flies settle on food. Therefore, food must be kept covered at all times. Spraying should kill them. Screen doors and windows can prevent their entry into the house. Fly swatter is another useful mechanism.

Crows: These are a nuisance and also spread germs if windows do not have a wire meshing. They do not hesitate to enter the house and feed on any food, which may have inadvertently, be kept on e.g., dining table or kitchen counter. The best way to keep them away is to have screen mosquito meshing on doors and windows.

Rats and mice: They are carriers of diseases like plague, typhus, food poisoning, jaundice and rat bite fever. They destroy food, clothing, draperies, upholstery, shrubs and trees. They breed in all seasons—4-7 times a year with litters of 6-22 that reach maturity in 100-120 days. It is essential to control rodents by rat proofing the house and ensuring that there are no entry points through which they can sneak in. Traps and poisons can be used but the rodents often evade these. An energetic and well fed cat often serves to eliminate these destructive creatures.

Stray cats and dogs: While stray cats can enter a house if windows do not have a meshing or grill, stray dogs do not normally enter a house. However, both are a nuisance and can be carriers of rabies. The gates and fencing of the house should be such that stray dogs are not able to enter. Cats, however, are more difficult to keep out as they can scale heights. An effective way of keeping them out is to seal garbage cans and ensure that no food is left outside.

Using Pesticides

Do's

- Read and follow the instructions and warnings on the package carefully.
- Mix pesticides in a well-ventilated area.
- While handling pesticides it is advisable to use rubber gloves.
- Keep pesticides in their original packaging, which should be tightly sealed and clearly labelled to avoid accidents.
- Pesticides must be stored in a locked well-ventilated area away from heat and direct sunlight.
- Wrap empty containers in thick layers of newspaper before discarding them.
- Exhaust all gas from pressurised cans before disposing of.
- Remove food, utensils, pets and their dishes prior to spraying indoors.
- Darkening rooms before spraying is the most effective way of spraying cockroaches.

Don'ts

- Don't use pesticides near children or pets.
- Don't smoke, eat or drink or chew gum.
- Avoid strong pesticides near food.
- Don't dump pesticides in places where they could endanger fish or wild life or contaminate water.

- Don't re-enter a room for half an hour after it has been sprayed.
- Close doors and windows after spraying a room.

Security

Old timers say that doors and windows were never locked in earlier times and gates were always kept open. The incidence of petty thefts and burglary were apparently less in the earlier decades of the century in this country, probably because of a greater awe and fear of the law enforcing authorities. Today, although India is a relatively safer country than many of our counterparts in the western world, given the sheer numbers of our people and the disparities between the haves and the have-nots, the time has nevertheless come for us to be more alert to security in our domestic sphere.

While the police is expected to keep the law and order machinery in such a manner that crime is kept under control, it is nevertheless incumbent on the householder and apartments, societies to make provision for security. At the village level, there is very little protection as the houses are mainly mud-huts. Moreover, earlier on there was a system of village chowkidars and the entire village being protected by gates. The same system of gates has now been introduced in Delhi in an attempt to make the neighbourhood secure.

Personal Safety and Security Measures

The Delhi police have issued certain do's and don'ts to maintain personal safety and to have certain basic security measures.

Do's

a) Put effective barring mechanisms on doors and windows, such as iron grills.

b) Put a magic eye on the door.

c) If possible, keep a dog as a pet.

d) Keep fit and alert.

e) Always go out in a group for an evening or morning walk.

f) Connect your neighbour's house and your home with an alarm bell.

g) Keep vital telephone numbers for emergencies.

h) Inform your nearest PCR Van and neighbours if you are suspicious of someone.

i) Get your servant or attendant verified at the nearest police station.

j) Ensure that all doors, especially the main entrance of the house has grills and proper locks. An electronic alarm system will also be of help.

k) Neighbourhood watch scheme for more interaction with the neighbours.

Don'ts

a) Don't leave valuables lying around in the house.

b) Don't make an ostentatious display of cash and jewellery.

c) Don't trust strangers and open your doors to unidentified people.

d) Don't be a recluse, keep socialising and be in touch with neighbours.

e) Don't ignore any suspicious incident. Inform the police.

f) Don't let your servant have an access to your almirah, safe, bank passbooks, etc.

g) Don't talk about family secrets/property in front of strangers/servants.

h) If alone at home don't open the door, preferably talk through the grill door.

Murders have taken place in high rise buildings also, highlighting the fact that people living in apartments are like sitting ducks waiting to be attacked by the assailant. Apart from the failure of the police in providing security to those staying in residential apartments, the private security system also seems to fail frequently. The police wash their hands off the security aspect in apartments by stating that the residential associations should keep private security guards or agencies. The apparent disinterest of the police coupled with the failure of private security makes people living in apartments more vulnerable to attacks by robbers and murderers. With the extra onus being on private security guards, police patrolling is rare in the jungle of concrete apartments which have mushroomed in many of our cities. With the neighbourhood watch scheme system missing in the majority of residential colonies, a lone security guard stationed at the colony gates with a register and stick in his hands cannot be expected to provide security to the hundreds of residents living inside. Since nuclear families are the order of the day and as neighbours are not really interested in what is happening in the flat next door, each person in an apartment is left to fend for himself, interaction among residents being at the bare minimum.

Making Doors and Windows Foolproof

Doors and windows must be made foolproof so that intruders do not have easy access to a house or apartment. Usually apartments have two entry points, i.e. a front door and a back door. Hence these must be kept securely locked at all times. There should either be a magic eye or a safety chain (preferably both) so that one can ascertain the identity of the caller before opening the door. A double door in which there is a wooden door as well as a door with wire meshing on the inside helps greatly as it makes it possible to see and talk to visitors without opening the door. At night, doors and windows should be properly shut and secured with bolts. Grills on the windows are also deterrents to intruders. Independent houses have many doors which make them less secure. One should try to limit the number of entry and exit points to two, i.e. a back door and a front door to make the house safer.

Types of Alarms

Due to the increase in crimes like theft and break-ins many types of safety alarms are available in the market. Some of these are electronic while others operate on a battery system. Depending on one's needs, these are a worthwhile investment.

Safety Lock

Safety locks for doors and windows are available in the market. These are expensive but make access to the house more difficult for intruders, e.g. in foreign countries there is an electronic burglar alarm which the householder switches on before leaving the house. In some farm houses and in other residential accommodation, people often use an electrical fencing whereby any person attempting to scale the fence will get an electric shock.

The Use of Manpower

Security agencies employ personnel who are specially trained and also certified by the police to work as security guards. Normally they work on a shift system and are rotated so that they do not develop vested interest in any particular place. The presence of such guards often acts as a deterrent to intruders. Some people also employ their own chowkidars or watchmen who are armed with sticks and are expected to maintain vigil on the house, especially at night.

Security Check of Domestic Help

Although domestic servants are a part of our lives in India, unfortunately, it has been seen that this class is more often than not involved in cases of burglary, theft and even assault, particularly on elderly people. If the antecedents of the domestic servant are not properly verified, he or she may commit a theft and then vanish to their far-off villages. Therefore, the police insist that in the interest of employers, they should have these domestic help verified by them. This implies that their photograph, name of the village, address are registered with the police so that they can be traced easily in case of any untoward incident.

Safety Guidelines

For the home

1. Lock all the doors while going out and install slam-shut doors in preference to padlocks. Leave one light on in the house while going out.
2. When going out of town, lock each room in addition to the main door of the house and ask your neighbours to keep a watch.
3. Do not open the door without first ascertaining the identity of the caller through the magic eye and always keep the door-chain in place when accepting mail or parcels.
4. Keep the door bolted even during the day.
5. A safe neighbourhood ensures a safe home, be an alert neighbour and watch out for suspicious people.
6. Apart from magic eyes and door chains, install iron grills, burglar alarms and car alarms.
7. Do not open cupboards in front of servants or unknown visitors.

8. Do not hire masons, plumbers, white washers etc. without verification.
9. When going out of town inform the local police, beat constable or watchman of your area. Tell the newspaper vendor not to deliver papers.
10. Do not let strangers in, even for a glass of water.

For the car

A large number of vehicle thefts can be checked if the car owners take the following precaution:

1. The owner or authorised driver of the car should not leave the vehicle unattended without locking the ignition and removing the key. A significant number of automobiles are stolen because drivers fail to remove ignition keys.
2. All members of the family should know how to protect the car against theft. Licences, registration cards or other identification papers that a thief could misuse should never be left in the car. The documents can be used to sell the vehicle or to impersonate the owner if the thief is challenged by the police.
3. Keys should be carefully guarded. If the keys have punchout numbers, these should be removed and kept at home for reference in case of loss.
4. Park in a well-lighted area.
5. Close all windows, lock all doors.
6. Activate any theft deterrent device you may have.
7. Put packages or valuables out of sight. Tapes and cassette decks and other expensive items in full view invite theft.
8. If you have a garage, use it. Lock both the vehicle and the garage.
9. Install auto-theft security devices. In case the car alarm goes off, observe

behaviour around the car, inform the police. Do not take direct action, your safety is of primary concern.

10. Etch the vehicle registration number in several hard-to-find spots using an engraving tool. In case such a vehicle is stolen and recovered, identification is made easy even if licence plates are altered and the vehicle is repainted.

11. If your car gets stolen, report to the police. (Note: false reporting of vehicle theft is a punishable crime.)

12. Proper maintenance of vehicles prevent breakdowns thus avoiding vulnerable situations.

For handling cash

The following safety precautions should be taken while handling cash:

- All transactions should be kept secret.
- Avoid withdrawal/deposit from the bank at fixed time and date.
- Avoid particular fixed route while carrying out business with bank.
- Avoid carrying cash alone or on foot. There should be sufficient number of persons for safety of cash.
- Avoid hiring taxi/TSR for the transportation of large amount. Use own transport.
- Avoid carrying large amount on two-wheelers.
- Carry a licensed weapon while carrying out transaction with bank.
- The money should be kept in a proper cavity in the vehicle or camouflaged.
- In case of suspicion of being followed, seek police or public help.
- Mobile phone should be carried for seeking timely help.
- Do not converse with strangers while carrying out bank transactions.

- Remain alert and observant during bank transactions.
- Do not get tricked by cheats who may tell you about petty currency notes on the floor inside or outside the bank.
- Payment of huge amount should be taken in a safe/ secured room of the bank.
- Only a secure bag or briefcase should be used for carrying cash in public places.

Safeguard Against Purse Snatching

- Do not carry a bag that makes you a target. A bag that dangles from the shoulder can be easily yanked off. On the other hand, bags that act as handcuffs injure women, as they don't come off easily.
- Be aware of your surroundings and carry your bag close to the body, tucked in at the elbow bend.
- Carry minimum cash, credit cards. Divide the money between pockets of the bag.
- If you are a victim of purse snatch, do not fight to hold on to your bag, as the snatcher could be armed with a weapon.

For the elderly

These special guidelines for senior citizens can help in making them less vulnerable:

1. The beat constable should survey the residence and point out the vulnerable spots and help block loopholes.

2. To help in an emergency, senior citizens should consider installing a distress alarm or a panic button or even a hooter.

3. Residents should realise their social responsibility and neighbours should adopt the senior citizen in their locality.

4. Senior citizens should not keep too many valuables in the house and these should not be displayed in the open.

5. Ostentation is likely to attract the attention of unsavoury characters and should be avoided.

For women

1. When coming home late at night, avoid shortcuts that are not well travelled or well lit.

2. Know the proprietors of reputed neighbourhood stores which are open late in the night and if you feel you are being followed, go there.

3. When walking to your car or on your way home, keep your keys in your hand till you are safely inside.

4. If someone drops you home, ask them to wait till you are inside.

5. If a motorist bothers you while you are walking, turn around and walk in the opposite direction.

6. While driving alone keep your windows rolled up and doors locked.

7. If someone attempts to force you off the road, don't panic, blow your horn constantly to attract attention. If you are forced to stop, put the car in reverse and back away as soon as possible. Keep your hand on the horn and the car in motion.

8. If you are being followed, make a few turns down active streets if possible. If the vehicle continues to follow you, head for the nearest police station, fire house or open store. Don't try to make it to your own quiet residential area.

9. Park your car in a well-lit area.

10. Before getting into your car, look inside first to make sure that no one is hiding in it. Make sure your car is locked when you leave it.

11. If you are alone at home, have your key ready before you get to the front door.

12. If a stranger wants to use your phone for any kind of emergency, keep him out and make the call yourself.

13. If you arrive home and find your door open, do not go inside. Call the police from a payphone or a neighbour's house.

For children

Guard against these common hazards.

BUCKETS

Babies often hold buckets, look in and reach out for their reflection. If they topple, their head weight instantly makes them plummet down.

Prevention:

If you must store water in a bucket, lock the room. Never leave a child alone near a filled bucket. And keep empty buckets upside down.

DRUGS & POISONS

Prevention:

1. Never leave drugs or household poisons within reach of children.

2. Some pills are easily mistaken for sweets, and kerosene kept in colourless bottles looks just like water. Store kerosene in cans or dark bottles, and keep it well out of reach of children.

BURNS

Prevention:

1. Most accidents at home take place in the kitchen. Children should never be allowed to use the stove and if there's a toddler in the house, remember to keep all hot liquids safely out of reach.

2. Diwali is a time when the incidence of burns among children rises sharply. Small children should never be allowed to handle fireworks.

3. Keep an eye on older children too. They should never play with fireworks inside the house, or when wearing loose-flowing clothes. Fireworks that fizzle out or don't explode should be doused with water.

ELECTRIC SHOCKS

Prevention:

1. Ensure all your electrical appliances are in good condition. Immediately discard those that are worn out.

2. Place dummy plugs over all unused electrical sockets.

3. Have an electrician install residual current circuit breakers (RCCBs) in your home. An RCCB (also called ELCB, for earth leakage circuit breaker) instantaneously cuts off power when there is any leakage of current, as when somebody gets a shock. Although the Indian Electricity Rules make RCCBs mandatory only in places that consume five kilowatts or more of power, every home should have them.

Falls

Prevention:

1. If you live on an upper floor, check that your balcony railings and grills aren't of the kind that children can climb.

2. Windows should also be fitted with fixed grills so that there's no way children can fall out.

3. Do not keep chairs, tables or stools on balconies, kids are sure to climb on them.

4. And never stand at the edge of a balcony holding a baby.

UNSAFE TOYS

Prevention:

1. Small children should never be given flimsy toys with small parts that can come off.

2. Even peanuts, button cells, coins and balloons pose major risks.

3. Young children have little control over their swallowing.

SCHOOL BUSES

Prevention:

1. Teach your child to walk slowly and carefully into his bus and to wait well away from it (never behind it, where the driver can't see), until a teacher or helper asks him to board.

2. Sometimes neither teachers nor helpers take care, it's vital that children be made aware of the dangers.

3. Make children understand that getting a front or window seat isn't important.

4. And that rushing into a bus can be very risky.

KIDNAPPING AND CHILD ABUSE

1. Instruct your child never to go off with strangers even if they are offered sweets and toffees.

2. Never to go off with anyone who is saying that your father or mother has sent for you if the person is unknown.

3. Always try to raise an alarm.

4. Instruct your child, irrespective of whether it is a boy or girl against immoral advances towards them even if it is a relative, friend or servant.

5. Parents should make foolproof arrangements when children go to school and when they return.

■■

CHAPTER-3

Maintaining the House

The Exterior

The exterior of the house is subject to a great deal of weathering. It also forms the first impression of the house.

While, some houses have the exterior of stone, open brick or marble tiles, the most common in India is the one of cement plaster. Painting the exterior is highly expensive and therefore, the paint used should be such that it stays for at least 3 years, if not more.

Checking the roof

The roof of the house must be checked periodically to ensure that cracks do not develop as these cracks will result in leakages during the heavy monsoon rains in our country. One also has to check the roof to

ensure that small plants have not taken root as these would cause cracks to develop. The roofs should have projecting pipes through which excess rain water drains out. One should check the roof particularly before the monsoons to ensure that these defects have not cropped up. The water storage tank on top of the house should have a bab-cock system and should be kept covered to guard against birds, insects, etc. from falling in. The bab-cock should function to ensure that water does not leak out as constant leakages would cause damage to the roof.

Repairing cracks

Today, many durable adhesive mixtures are available for repairing cracks on the roofs. One should not try to cut corners by using cheaper materials.

Plumbing

The plumbing systems in the house especially sewage lines need to be checked by a plumber and sanitation expert periodically.

The electrical outlets connecting the internal connections of the house to the electricity board lines should also be checked at regular intervals against wear and tear.

Telephone connections come into the house from an external pole. If this wire is loose, cut or damaged in any way the phone connection is affected. Therefore, the proper maintenance of this line is essential.

The Interior

How often should rooms be painted?

There is no strict rule on how often rooms should be painted. Some paint their rooms as often as once a year while others do not undertake this inconvenience for years together. In India paint rather than wall paper is the norm and due to our vast manpower, painting the house is entrusted to professionals rather than the self help method necessitated in the west. The cost of painting the room depends on the quality and category of paint used. While ordinary white wash is inexpensive but not long lasting, oil based washable paints are quite expensive. As getting the rooms painted while one is living in is a mammoth task, it may be done once in two-three years. Due to the high percentage of pollution in the air and dust and dirt particles in the house, it is advisable to paint the interiors within this time frame so that excessive scrapping is not necessitated. It is best to paint the interiors after the monsoons so that any damp patches which may have developed can be repaired and painted over. As far as possible it is best not to paint the house during the monsoons and winter in the northern part of India as the humidity and extreme cold make it difficult for the paint to dry quickly.

Why are paints used?

Our homes are made up of wood, metal, cement, bricks and many other materials and over a period of time the beauty and strength of these get decreased. Walls crack and chip, metals rust and corrode and wooden parts warp and scratch. Paints form a protective layer over these surfaces. They do not allow them to get weathered or affected by other external factors. In short, paints keep them looking as good as new.

WALLS

The kinds of paint available for walls are sold under many brand names but are of the following types:

Emulsions: These are water based paints. Acrylic Emulsions are extremely durable and give walls a matty, smooth finish. They are washable and are therefore easy to maintain.

Distempers: These are also water based paints. But their binders may be natural or synthetic. Distempers are economically priced and offer good value for money as they are very durable. Another type of distemper also available in the market is Synthetic Distemper. It is offered as the lower end product in distemper category and can last for one year.

EXTERIOR FINISHES

For exteriors, cement paint is most commonly used as it is economical. However, its resistance to fungus and algae is relatively low. The available alternatives are given below.

Texturised exterior finishes with sand finish.

100% Acrylic exterior emulsion paint.

For high performance and protection of exterior walls against fungus, algae and mould growth, one can go in for either Texturised exterior finishes or 100% Acrylic exterior emulsions depending on the budget.

SURFACES

The best coating for metals is provided by synthetic enamels. Also, available are paints that are specially developed for particular metals.

METALS

Synthetic enamels provide the best coating for metals. They are tough, durable and glossy in finish. Enamels protect metals from corrosion. Synthetic Enamels are also used for wooden surfaces like doors, windows, furniture, etc. since they give longer life to the wood. However, they do not retain the original beauty of the wood. Synthetic Enamels generally come in 3 grades: First, Second and Third quality.

WOOD

When painting wood, there is a choice between covering the surface with an opaque coating like enamel or bringing out the natural beauty of the wood grain with a clear transparent finish.

Transparent finishes for wood are of the following types:

Melamine based finishes: These are superior transparent finishes that enhance the natural beauty of wood. They are tough, scratch and stain resistant.

Primers: Other than actual paints, you will also need to purchase primer suitable for the surface to be painted. Primers are as important as paints as they provide the basis of a good paint job.

A few words of advice

- Rectify any existing surface problems such as dampness and crack before painting.
- Thinners, primers and undercoats should be of good quality. Though most painters would suggest the use of low quality ones, you must insist on buying these from major paint companies to get the full range of good quality. These provide the foundation of any beautifully finished surface.
- Make sure the surface is clean and free from dust, loose particles and grease before painting.

- Remove rust and scale from metals using a wire brush or sandpaper.
- Test the paint on a small area on the wall before buying the full quantity.
- Make sure you have enough paint for the job before starting work.
- Stir and strain paints thoroughly before application. Most paints settle to a certain extent in the can. The paint should also be thinned properly to ensure adequate application viscosity.
- Buy readymade shades as far as possible. Mixing and tinting of shades done by painters may give you different results from wall to wall. However, if you buy tinted shades through computerised colour dispensers, you can be sure of consistent shades as you would get in the case of readymade shades.
- Leftover paints can be used innovatively— paint a motif on the wall, paint a stool or a door.
- It is not advisable to paint in humid conditions. Avoid painting in the monsoons as the paint takes long time to dry and the film will not cure properly.
- The room to be painted should be well ventilated and free from dust.
- Always clean spilt or splashed paint with the recommended thinner while it is still wet.
- To guarantee a neat edge around window panes, protect the glass with paint shield or apply masking tape before painting. Remove it before the final coat is dry to avoid peeling a layer of paint off.
- Always allow the paint to overlap slightly on the glass to prevent moisture

from seeping to the joint between putty and glass.

- When spraying paint, mask other surfaces around the area with newspaper or plastic to protect them.

- Wear a mask while rubbing down paint surface.

- Do not breathe vapour/spray.

- Keep paint away from food, drink and animal feed. As far as possible, use water-based paints for your interiors to make the process of painting comfortable to the people living.

- Wear eye protection masks when painting. In case of contact with eye, rinse thoroughly with water and seek medical advice.

Some maintenance tips

Like painting once in 2-3 years gives a new look to the wall, maintaining the painted surfaces is also necessary to give a good look. Take some time at least once in a month for this activity.

- To remove stains and dust from a painted surface, use a clean white cloth or a sponge, dipped in a mild detergent solution. After cleaning, wash away all traces of detergent and wipe dry.

- Never use water for spot cleaning unless the wall is totally free from extraneous dust.

- For distempered walls, minimum pressure should by applied while cleaning.

- Enamel surfaces should be cleaned with a detergent solution and immediately wiped dry. Never use thinners to clean enamel painted surfaces.

- If paint on metal or steel furniture is damaged, have it touched up immediately with primer and paint to avoid rusting.

- The recommendations for wood given above are for clear wood finishes. If one wishes to have coloured finishes, synthetic enamels in third or second or first quality can be chosen depending on the budget.

- For metals to obtain silver coloured finishes, aluminium paints can be applied in first or second quality after thorough preparation by metal primers.

- With medium budget, one can also get walls done with lustre finish instead of plastic/ acrylic emulsion.

Coping with damp patches

Whenever damp patches develop they normally do so in the corner of the ceiling of the rooms, below windows or at any point where pipes are running through the wall, e.g. in the wall between a bedroom and bathroom. Adequate measures such as re-plastering should be done after ascertaining the cause for their occurrence so that they do not recur.

Ensuring electrical safety

Due to the threat of electrical short circuit and the danger of electrocution specially with children in the house, utmost priority must be given to electrical safety. No expense should be spared to ensure the best quality of electrical wiring, switches and safety devices, such as childproof switches. Low plug points should either be capped up or covered by a piece of furniture so that children are not attracted by the empty holes of the plug points into which they may be tempted to insert either their finger or any other pointed object.

For heavy equipment, such as air conditioners, refrigerators, geysers and room heaters, a suitable MCB switch should be installed. The proper earthing of wires and the safety of the fuse boxes should be ensured. If a fuse blows, the cause of the fault should be ascertained rather than putting in a heavier fuse

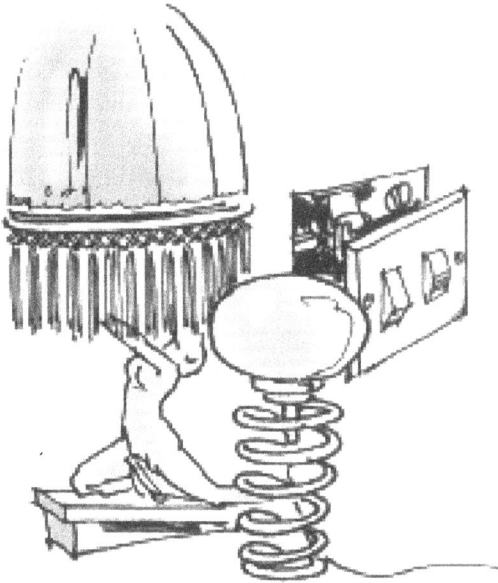

so that the fuse does not blow out. It should be remembered that the fuse blowing is indicative of some fault in the line which should be attended to promptly by a reliable electrician. It is best to employ the services of one electrician who is familiar with the wiring of the house rather than getting help from different people whenever the need arises.

Nobody can afford to be complacent about the electrical safety of their home. Most defects are in plugs, flexes and fuses and can result in fire or serious electric shocks. Thus, 'weak line' which melts and cuts off the current if the circuit is overloaded is often replaced by tin wires too thick to melt. Many faulty socket outlets are broken, exposing live parts which could kill anybody who touches them. Wrongly connected or defective electrical appliances such as refrigerators, washing machines and immersion heaters are used in kitchens and bathrooms where water and damp floors increase the possibility of

electrocution. Have a look at every plug in your own home. Does it bear the ISI stamp? Those without this government seal of reliability should be replaced. Don't use two-pin plugs. These lack an earth terminal and are forbidden under the Indian Electricity Rules. Now check that the plug's case is not cracked or broken. Unscrew the cover and check that the wires are connected correctly, the green wire to the earth terminal at the top, the live brown or red wire to the terminal on the right, the black or blue neutral wire to the terminal on the left. If the live and neutral wires are reversed, the appliance at the other end of the flex may be 'live' even when it is apparently switched 'off.' And if the 'live' and earth wires are reversed, and the fuse does not blow, any metal part in an appliance will be 'live.'

With a screwdriver, make sure that the terminals hold the wires firmly. Loose connections cause sparks and overheating. Cut away any stray wisps of wire and shake them out of the plug. Even a single strand could lead to tragedy.

Criminal Negligence: Make sure the cord grip holds the flex firmly. Otherwise a tug may drag the wire from its terminals. If that happens to the earth wire, the appliance will still work but it will be a potential killer.

Examine all socket outlets for fractures and replace those that are faulty. Ask an electrician to check that your sockets are properly earthed. It's not uncommon for unscrupulous electrical contractors to cut corners and not provide proper earthing. Using water pipes for earthing is dangerous, since in many modern buildings water pipes are not buried in the ground. In theory, government electricity inspectors are required to check and certify the safety of all new wiring. But unfortunately, in practice even such criminal negligence is often winked at – for a price.

The bathroom can be an efficient death chamber, as several murderers have proved by dropping live electrical appliances into baths containing their victims. Geysers, especially the instant types, should be permanently fixed (with outside or pull-cord ceiling switches). You should not use an electric *sigree*, hair-dryer or other portable appliances in a bathroom. The only advisable outlet is a shaver socket with a built-in transformer.

If you think your bathroom fittings are not safe, have them replaced or removed immediately. Tomorrow may be too late. Bathrooms and kitchens are potentially the most dangerous places in your homes, but there are hazards wherever there is electricity. Follow these points:

- If an electric iron or any other appliance has too much flex, resist the temptation to coil it. Shorten the flex so that it does not get damaged and overheated, perhaps causing a short circuit and fire.

- Never join two lengths of flex together with coloured adhesive insulation tape. It's not safe. Use flex of the correct length instead. Make sure all plugs fit snugly in the socket.

- If you hear a whirring or a crackling sound in the plug or the appliance, switch it off immediately. It means there is a fault somewhere. Often fires start from flashing, sparking and short circuits in wiring.

- Watch the flex feeding an electric iron or a table lamp. Constant rubbing on a table or ironing-board wears away the insulation and in time exposes the bare wires.

- Switch off appliances at the socket, and, just in case the socket switch is faulty, play doubly safe and take the plug out at night. Do this with all appliances when you go away on a holiday or switch off at the mains.

- Don't move an appliance around while it is connected to a socket.

- If the radiant electric fire does not have a guard angled so that the live element cannot be touched, get one made.

- Don't rig up makeshift electrical equipment, even temporarily.

- If you're using an immersion heater, switch it off before testing the water with your finger. Otherwise, you may get a shock.

- Unless the current carrying capacity of the wires permit it, don't use more than one appliance from one socket. The wires could overheat and start a fire.

- If possible, locate all sockets at a height above the reach of children. Otherwise, secure sockets with 3-pin plugs.

What about all the wires you can't see-- those buried behind plaster, under the floors and above your ceilings? If they are more than 25 years old, they may need replacing. The danger signs are fuses which frequently blow and sockets which become hot. During the rainy season, water may seep into the walls and damage the wiring inside. And once the insulating material is damaged, you can get a shock merely from touching a wet wall. Waterproof all walls exposed to heavy rain. In particular, terraces—where water often accumulates—should be waterproofed or at least given a tar coating before every monsoon.

A licensed electrical contractor will give your wiring a visual check and an estimate of the cost of putting things right. Get estimates from at least three firms licensed for wiring.

Silent, invisible, odourless, electricity is a wonderful servant, but a deadly master. There's no need to be scared of it. It is ready to work for you but, if you abuse it, it can kill you. Treat it with the greatest respect.

Maintenance of doors

Doors should be maintained as they guard the security of the house. The locks should be functional and all doors must close properly. Latches and keys should fit. In case of hinges, grease or oil should be applied. If done so regularly, the noise is taken care of.

Maintenance of windows

Windows should be opened everyday and should also be shut fully. Broken glass panes should be replaced immediately. Window fasteners should be in place to ensure that windows do not slam on their own.

Maintenance of pelmets

Pelmets carry the weight of curtains which are pulled and tugged at everyday. Therefore, one must ensure that pelmets are properly fixed to the wall. The traditional wooden pelmets have been replaced in many homes with curtain rods which are easier to maintain. Pelmets should be painted and polished when the room is painted. Pelmets should normally be painted brown so that they blend with the walls and do not attract attention. Rather the focus of attention should be on the curtains.

Care for Your Appliances

Audio system

Protect from dust.

Use good quality cassettes for better life of the audio-head.

Clean audio-head with standard head cleaner from time to time.

For cleaning the lens of CD player, do not use wet cleaner, use either CD-lens cleaner or ask your concerned service technician.

Air conditioner

Cleaning the filter: Ensure the unit is off before taking off the filter. Clean the filter using a vacuum cleaner or in tap water. Do not use chemical solvents for cleaning. Shake the filter dry. Slide it back into the unit after cleaning.

Clean once every fifteen days or more depending upon the operating conditions. Ensure that the filter is kept clean. It ensures enhanced cooling, lower power consumption and increased unit life.

Cleaning the unit: Periodically clean the unit with a soft cloth dampened with mild detergent, thereafter wipe clean with a dry cloth. Do not use bleaching powder, hot water, thinner or petrol for cleaning. Ensure the power to the unit is off while cleaning.

Service and maintenance: Get your unit serviced regularly from an approved service technician. This is essential for the optimum functioning of the unit and will ensure enhanced unit life and performance. Do not attempt servicing your unit yourself as it can be hazardous due to system pressure and electrical components.

After-season care of the unit: Clean the filter before putting off the unit till the next season. Disconnect power supply to the unit. On a sunny day, operate the unit on 'fan mode' for half day to clean the unit interior.

Precautions: Use the correct voltage. Using voltage other than specified will damage the unit. Install a voltage stabilizer. Check the power plug. If the power plug is not inserted tightly or if there is any damage to the power cord, it could result in leakage or electrical shock.

Use only correct fuses of proper amperage. If using rewirable fuse, use only the correct fuse wire as fire or an electrical accident may occur. Do not put hand or objects into the supply air grill of the unit. These units have a blower running at high speed.

When unplugging the power plug, do not pull it by the power cord. The power cord will be damaged and it will cause electrical shock.

To avoid the risk of serious electrical shock, never wash the unit with water.

Do not obstruct the front of discharge grill. This will block air flow, reduce the cooling effect, and may cause unit malfunction.

Do not use flammable sprays near the unit. The unit can be damaged by gasoline, thinners and other such chemicals.

Do not clean the unit with thinner, hot water or chemicals, use soft cloth dampened with mild detergent.

Before cleaning, ensure that the power supply to the unit is off.

Ensure that the 'activate timer' function is off when you do not require timer function, so that the timer programme does not on/off the unit when not required. When the unit is not in use and timer function is not required, switch off the electrical supply to the unit.

Generator

- Check fuel level before starting.
- Stop engine before filling fuel.
- Filter the fuel before filling into the tank.
- Keep inflammable matter away (1 metre).

- Check engine oil level before each start.
- Use recommended engine oil.
- Change engine oil, first 20 hours of use. Afterwards every 100 hours of use.
- Use choker for cold starting.
- Always connect through changeover switch.
- Switch on appliances drawing higher current first.
- Follow maintenance schedule.
- Always use genuine spares.
- Never connect two or more gensets.
- Never fill less or more engine oil.
- Never connect directly to household wiring.
- Genset should be used inside an enclosed area. Ensure adequate ventilation while genset is in operation.
- Do not put a dust cover while genset is in operation.
- Do not use in wet surroundings.
- Do not touch the genset with wet hands.
- Do not connect pipe to exhaust pipe.
- Do not spill fuel while pouring.

Refrigerator

Follow the manufacturer's instructions to defrost. Generally a chart is provided giving the frequency of defrosting during the various seasons.

The thermostat setting for the different climates are given. As a thumb rule, keep the thermostat at minimum during the winter months and normal during other months. In peak summer, the efficiency is reduced, especially in very hot climates, making it necessary to turn the thermostat to the maximum level.

Periodic cleaning of the interior and exterior of the refrigerator is important to keep up the efficiency of cooling. At least once a fortnight, switch off the refrigerator and remove the plug from the socket. Remove all the contents and take out the racks and the glass cover of the vegetable tray.

Use a liquid soap or one of those cleaning liquids available for this purpose. Spray it and wipe down with a soft cloth. If you are using soap and water, soak a sponge in soap water, squeeze it out and wipe with it. Remove the soap with a wet cloth. You can wash the racks and trays with soap water. Dry well before restoring the contents of the refrigerator. Clean the coils with a duster to remove the dust.

Avoid putting heavy things on the bridge. Spread a cloth or plastic sheet on the top to prevent scratches.

Find out if your refrigerator has a built-in stabilizer and its range. Refrigerators of well-known brands have this feature. If it does not, buy an external stabilizer.

Keep the refrigerator away from moisture and heat.

Washing machine

Washing machines are available in a variety of models. The costliest being the front-loading tumble-wash model which is fully automatic. Next in range comes the top-loading fully-automatic models, then the twin-tub semi-automatic model and finally the washer, which only washes and rinses the clothes.

For practical purposes, the twin-tub semi-automatic model is quite good enough. Though it requires your presence from time to time, it is very efficient. The latest models have the rinse cycle in the dryer itself and consumes much less water than if you were to rinse in the washer. A washing machine is usually quite sturdy and does not give much trouble, but do keep it clean and dry after use. See that the point where you plug in is earthed to prevent shocks.

Vacuum cleaner

It is very useful in cleaning carpets, upholstered sofas, heavy curtains, removing cobwebs, cleaning electronic appliances, etc. Though it does not mop up the floor, it is useful when there are no servants. Vacuuming twice or thrice a week is enough to get the house really clean. A variety of brands are available to choose from.

The various attachments that come with the vacuum cleaner take care of virtually all your cleaning needs. You can dust upholstery, beds, valuable electronic equipment, the cobwebs, fans, etc.

Clean the outer surface of the vacuum cleaner with a sponge soaked in soap water. Take care to see that no water enters the appliance. The dust bag can be changed when the indicator shows that it is full.

Room heater

Compact convection heaters with a blower or fan are the best. These come in both vertical and horizontal models and have automatic temperature and speed controls.

Never leave a room heater on in the children's room the whole night. Switch it off after a couple of hours.

Never close all the doors and windows of the room when you are running a heater. The temperature can become uncomfortable and cause suffocation.

The room becomes very dry due to loss of moisture and can aggravate colds and coughs.

One method of preventing this is to keep a bowl of hot water in front of the heater.

Do not keep the heater on a metal surface.

If you do buy the open coil type of heater, keep it out of reach of small children.

Room coolers

They are less expensive than air conditioners. They work best in the months preceding the monsoons. They consume less electricity than air conditioners and their maintenance is more or less hassle free. Before buying a local brand check out the following:

How to place a cooler

Fix the cooler on a window, from the outside so that evaporation takes place and the cooling is better.

If you are using a desert cooler, select a window or outlet that faces the entire house. This way, the cool air gets circulated throughout the house.

See that there is proper arrangement for filling water.

Coolers that have wheels can be moved from place to place as needed.

How to place a water heater

Wherever there is running water or at least stored water that can be piped, water heaters can be used. Storage water heaters are available from 10 litres to 50 litres. For a family of four members, 25 litres capacity heater is enough. Instant geysers are those where running water gets heated as it passes through the heating coils in the geyser.

These come in sizes ranging from one litre to five litres. The disadvantage of this type of geyser is that hot water cannot be saved and running water is a must. If the water stops, there is danger of overheating and subsequent accidents due to it.

When you fix a storage type heater, select the shape and size according to the size of the bathroom as well as your family. A bathroom where the ceiling is low would do well with a horizontal heater. Similarly, you can buy either a cylindrical or squarish heater depending upon the bathroom and personal preference.

In the storage heater too, the source of the water should be running. You cannot remove the water from a storage heater if the overhead tank which feeds it is empty or if the municipal water supply has stopped. Your plumber will advise you in this matter.

Zinc, brass and copper drums fitted with a heater coil are also used. They have a tap which can be opened for hot water. The danger with these heaters is that they can give nasty shocks if there is some leakage.

Immersion heater

Wherever it is not feasible to have a water heater, an immersion heater is valuable. Copper ones are best as they conduct heat very fast. These are available in 1000, 1500 and 2000 watts rating. Usually, 1000 watts heaters are goo enough, but where there is a power problem or when you need water quickly, you can buy one of the higher wattage ones. Check with your electrician to see that the power outlet is capable of taking the excess load.

What to look for in a mixer-grinder

While buying a mixer-grinder, see that the wattage of the motor and its rating. Usually, the better quality mixer-grinders have a 30-45 minute rating.

Do not compromise on quality and buy local mixer-grinder, which burn out with the slightest load.

How to use the mixer-grinder

Put in only quantities specified in the instruction booklet. Never overload the jar.

When grinding very small quantities, use the smaller jar attachment, powder the masala dry, even if you new wet masala because once you add water, the material is likely to stick to the walls of the jar and does not get ground properly.

When wet-grinding soaked dals or cereal, first let the food get ground a little before adding water. Add water little by little, pushing the matter sticking to the walls of the jar by a wooden or plastic spatula.

Care of your mixer-grinder

Never leave the jar of the mixer-grinder to dry after wet-grinding anything. Instead, clean it immediately with water and soap. Dry it instantly, since the central shaft that holds the blade can trap water or food particles and rust. This in turn will jam the blade shaft.

To clean the blade shaft of all its food particles, run the mixer-grinder with some water before removing the blade. This will effectively clean all crevices.

Do not leave the blade on the shaft after finishing grinding. Remove, clean and dry it thoroughly before putting it away.

Keep the mixer-grinders outer surface clean by sponging with a sponge soaked in soap water. Squeeze out the water and clean well. Clean with a clean wet cloth and then with a dry cloth. Use a brush to clean the air vents in the mixer-grinder to prevent clogging with dust.

Keep the mixer-grinder covered when not in use.

Sharpen the blades of the mixer-grinder by running a handful of salt through it at medium speed.

The Kitchen

The kitchen is unfortunately, usually a small part of the house but an average housewife spends a major part of her day over here. The furniture should be arranged in such a way that cooking and preparing meals is made convenient.

The natural work sequence in the kitchen, namely food storage, preparation, cooking, serving, washing up and clearing away is represented today by the refrigerator, cooking range and sink.

The refrigerator, sink and cooking stove or range compose the three work centres in the kitchen. The refrigerator can be placed next to the counter where vegetables are kept. Dishes and dish washing materials should be stored close to the sink. The serving counter should be next to the sink. This should be close to the dining room or serving window between the dining room and kitchen. The three major units, refrigerator, sink and cooking stove/range should ideally be in a triangular arrangement to facilitate handling by the housewife. There should be adequate space for the preparation of food. A wooden inset in the counter top could be provided for cutting and slicing vegetables.

Storage place for utensils should be near the space where they are used.

Kitchen counters and storage cabinets

Storage is a very important part of the kitchen so that all kitchen equipment can be kept conveniently. All things of daily use are stored in the lower shelves. The general principle in planning storage is to store supplies and utensils at their point of first use. Both base cabinets and wall cabinets may be used for this purpose.

Dish washing and cleaning equipment should be kept close to the sink. Clean towels and dish towels should be kept in shelves near the sink.

The garbage pail should be kept covered and placed under the sink.

The shelf for spices should be above the cooking range while the toaster and tea kettle should be kept near the serving space.

While the walls and floors of the kitchen should be tiled so that they can be cleaned easily, the counter should be either of granite, marble or Cudapa stone. The kitchen should have a safe electrical point so that gadgets such as the mixer, toaster, electric kettle, oven-toaster- grill, rice cooker, microwave oven and dish washer can be used.

The refrigerator should have its own power connection. A voltage stabilizer should also be provided for. This could be placed on a wooden plank. Some housewives may use a dish washer and deep freeze depending on their requirements.

The sink

The porcelain kitchen sinks are rapidly being replaced by stainless steel ones. Although this is initially more expensive it is also more durable and causes less damage to crockery during washing. The sink should preferably be connected to a geyser so that hot water can be used for washing.

Safety factor in the kitchen

Due to the presence of fire, safety factors in the kitchen are of the greatest importance. The gas cylinder should be placed in such a way that it is switched off after use. A movable round trolley facilitates easy movement of the cylinder. The height of the cooking counter should be such that it is neither too high nor too low for the housewife.

The modern kitchen uses gas or electricity. Since it becomes very hot, there is a need for just about the cooking area. Cooking smells, fumes and steam makes the kitchen suffocating and an "electrical chimney" or an exhaust fan is essential so that the smells and fumes do not spread to the rest of the house.

Cleanliness requirement

The kitchen should preferably have wire-meshing on the doors and windows so that flies, birds, cats, etc. do not have access. The kitchen must be swept and wiped even thrice a day so that it remains clean after cooking. The garbage pail must be emptied out and washed with dettol from time to time. The pail should also be kept covered at all times and could be lined with a garbage bag to facilitate easy cleaning. Regular fumigation at night and ensuring that no food stuff is left outside will reduce the threat from ants and cockroaches.

The kitchen is the window to our family's health and its cleanliness must be ensured at all costs.

How to wash

Cooking utensils require strong detergents so that the excess oil is removed. Wire scrub or scotch bright may be used for this purpose.

Melmoware on the other hand should not be scrubbed with a strong detergent and wire as they result in scratching the surface. Porcelain should be washed with sponge and can be placed on the plates rack so that it dries on its own. Storing these away when wet can result in water marks. Cutlery must also be washed with a sponge and detergent so that no food particles remain.

Ventilation and lighting

Ventilation and lighting in a kitchen are important. Windows should be kept open to allow free flow of air while the wire meshing will help to keep out insects and flies. The use of exhaust fan or chimney while cooking eliminates extra smoke. A ceiling fan is required but can be switched on when gas is not in use. Tubelights should be placed above the cooking area and at another convenient point depending on the size of the kitchen. There should also be provision for two bulb fixtures which will operate in case of low voltage.

Kitchen woes due to plumbing

"The drains are clogged" is a common complaint all housewives have when it comes to kitchens. In spite of regular care and cleaning of the lint trap of food residues and soap suds, drain flow somehow seems to slow down in a while.

1. Avoid pouring greasy substances down the drains.
2. Grease deposits that collect, nevertheless, may be dissolved by pouring boiling water alongwith washing soda down the drain on a regular basis.

3. It is also a good idea to keep a plunger or "Plumber's helper" handy for quick drain help.
4. However, try not to be too experimental where drains are concerned. Do not mix two different cleaners or use one cleaner after another unless the initial cleaner has been flushed away with gallons of water.
5. Desperate measures such as using a plunger immediately after a cleaner has been used, may cause chemical splash back, so be careful. It's best to call a plumber, when the going gets too messy.

Kitchen sinks

Kitchen sinks are yet another tiresome and possibly the most important areas in the kitchen that need constant maintenance and care. Somehow no matter how much you look after them, there is nothing you can do to prevent drain clogging or discolouration. Home remedies are often the most effective as in cleaning hard water deposits with a solution of white vinegar and water, or removing stains with a paste of lemon juice and borax powder. Cleaning procedures, of course depend largely on the material your sink is made of. If the fixtures are older, chances are the material is porcelain on cast iron, and they may not be as acid and alkaline resistant as the newer porcelain on steel sinks. Cultured marble is also used, and sometimes is moulded into the counter-top for an all-in-one look. Fibreglass marble is now getting more popular in new home construction and remodelling, but they are not nearly as durable as porcelain-coated steel, and need special care to avoid scratching. The most economical cleaning solution for porcelain as well as cultured marble and fibreglass fixtures is a home recipe consisting of

1/2 cup baking soda mixed in a gallon of hot water. However, do be cautioned that this is a highly powerful solution. So it is best to use rubber gloves. Just apply this solution to the areas to be cleaned, scrubbing a bit if necessary, and rinse well with clear water.

Kitchen Hardware

Be it in metal, ceramic or wood, kitchen hardware also need regular care. Faucets, tops, drain fixtures and rods are usually made of chromium or stainless steel. Of course, if your budget allows, you can indulge in brass/copper hardware or any other fancy fittings in antique or modern finish. A quick wipe with a sponge or cloth saturated with the cleaning agent you use is probably the fastest and best way to clean most hardware. Rinse well with clear water and buff shine with dry cloth. Otherwise, baking soda is the cheapest way to clean and polish aluminium and chrome surfaces. Sprinkle some powder on the wet surface making a paste, and use a synthetic scouring pad to spread it. Rinse and buff for a bright finish. Brass tarnishes when exposed to air benefits from a good cleaner/polish. However a paste made of 1 tablespoonful each of salt, flour and vinegar is the most economical method for cleaning brass. Applied with a cloth, the paste is very effective in making tarnish disappear and shine reappear. Dipping a cut lemon in salt and then rubbing it on brass surface is another quick and inexpensive way to clean brass. Be sure to wash in warm soap suds, and buff dry to bring back the shine.

Kitchen equipment

A plethora of high quality kitchen gadgets have ensured that a housewife's task is simplified more than ever. These appliances keep in mind the needs of a modern day woman who has to walk a tightrope between her house and workplace. These equipments are an excellent way to save time.

Liquidizer/blender: A liquidizer/blender is used for emulsifying ingredients for mayonnaise, dips and sandwich spreads. It is excellent for preparing milk shakes and fruit purees which can be poured straight into the serving jug or tumbler. One can buy attachments like a chutney or chopper jar in which small portions of boneless meat can be minced. This attachment can also be used to cut onions, green chillies, tomatoes and other vegetables that don't need uniform chopping. It is excellent for making purees from cooked vegetables or soft fruits for babies who are being weaned. The juicer attachment extracts juice from citrus fruits without crushing the pips.

Food processor: This gadget handles quantities that may be too much for a blender. Its various blades and discs shred, slice, chop and grate vegetables. The food processor also kneads dough for puris, paranthas and short-crust.

Freezer: The advantage of a freezer is that you can stock up on meats and blanched vegetables so that last minute shopping is unnecessary.

Microwave oven: A great advantage of a microwave oven is that it is automated and one doesn't need to keep watching the time. It's important to use the right containers in microwave ovens. Dishes should be shallow since the microwave cannot penetrate more than four centimetres. Microwaves do not heat food in metal or glass containers. Although some containers have 'microwave safe' marked on them, many don't.

If you want to know whether a container is microwave safe, place it inside the oven next to half a glass of water. Turn heat on high for one to one and a half minutes. If the container is cold then it's microwave safe, but if it's hot, it is not. For more efficient cooking, cover the food or container with plastic cling film.

Mixer-grinder: This is used to grind masalas, rice and dals. These days, mixer-grinders cum food processors are available.

OTGs: Oven-toaster-grills or OTGs are present in most homes. There is little to chose between brands—most are good.

Roti maker: Though it makes rolling pins and boards redundant, rotis made by this device cannot match the hand-made variety. It is excellent, however, for making low-calorie, non-fat rotis.

Tea and coffee makers: Since coffee makers are basically electric filters, they have not become widely popular as ground coffee is preferred only in the south.

Dishwasher: IFB and Videocon offer large-capacity dishwashers. This is a gadget worth investing in. Though the utensils that go on a cooking stove still need to be scrubbed first by hand, tableware comes out sparkling clean.

How to arrange appliances in a kitchen

See how big the kitchen platform is and where the sink is. Let us assume that the platform is on one side of the kitchen and is eight feet long. Use the space by the side of the gas stove to put finished dishes and for preparing the food - like making chapatis, cutting vegetables, etc. You can place a wire basket on one side of the sink to hold the washed vessels. A corner of the platform can house the mixer-grinder.

Keep the refrigerator on the opposite wall or to one side, if the room is big enough. Otherwise keep it in an adjoining room.

Try to keep the gas stove near a window

for ventilation and light. If you have poor ventilation in the kitchen, use an exhaust fan.

The shelves should be placed away from the gas stove. If you have shelves running above the stove, you may burn yourself when reaching for something on the shelf. Also, chances of oil stains and smoke spoiling the shelves and their contents are more.

Let the height of the shelves also be at a comfortable level. Keep frequently used items at shoulder height shelves and others at higher or lower levels. Use a small stool to reach upper shelves.

Put up the plate and spoon stands above the sink by nailing them to the wall. They will drip into the sink.

If you have covered shelves, well and good. Otherwise, arrange the tins and bottles in a beautiful manner, so that they do not look cluttered.

Always keep the kitchen bright. Use a tubelight fitting that reflects light in the cooking area. If you do not have a tubelight, at least go in for a 100 watt light bulb that hangs above the kitchen platform. Dark kitchens breed insects and other pests.

The Bathroom

Bathrooms were initially the most neglected part of an Indian house. Today greater attention is being placed on the bathrooms so that they may be well ventilated, easily accessible and aesthetic. While hotel rooms frequently have bathrooms in which there are no windows, a domestic bathroom must be placed in such a way that there is a window which provides adequate ventilation, as well as privacy to the user. In many of the bathrooms in the duplex houses in England, a single bathroom for as many as 3 bedrooms is placed on the landing of the staircase. Not only does this offer any privacy to the user but there is also very little ventilation to remove the steam and air.

The ideal arrangement in any house is to have one bathroom for each bedroom. In some flats, where there are two bathrooms an Indian style toilet is constructed separately from the

bathroom to reduce the pressure during rush hours. An area of 5 ft by 6 ft is quite adequate for a bathroom and 3 small bathrooms are better than having 2 large ones. Many people today prefer a bathing area with a shower and

taps rather than a tub, as these are generally difficult to keep clean and occupy a large area. These are also difficult for elders and children to get in and out of. A huge mirror, a wash basin with counters, a wall cabinet for toiletries and towel rails should be provided for. The space beneath the counter may either have shelving for storing towels etc. but due to the proliferation of cockroaches and the wood in these cabinets swelling up due to the constant humidity in the bathroom, many now prefer the space to be kept open so that buckets, waste paper baskets can be placed here. The container for clothes to be washed can also be kept here.

Electrical outlets in the bathroom for geysers, electric shavers and hair dryers may be placed above the counter.

Shower curtains are an effective way of keeping the floors dry. The bathroom floors should be kept dry and clean to avoid accidents. This can be achieved with the help of wipers. A fan in the bathroom also facilitates this. A grab or a grab bar in the shower area and next to the toilet are a help for all and are a must for the elderly.

High quality plumbing and equipment should be used in the bathroom as these are more cost-effective in the long run. During construction or when one enters a new home, one should ensure that the gradient of the floor is such that no water collects any where.

Doors and latches should be such that people do not get accidentally locked in. A door knob with an outside lock release would prevent children and elders from locking themselves in. Buckets and mugs should match the colour of tiling in the bathroom and should be cleaned periodically so that fungus does not collect. Shower curtains should also be cleaned from time to time.

■■

CHAPTER-4

A Guide to Home Decor

Everyone wants a dream-house and has done so since pre-historic times. In those days man had to build the house himself, but it was the woman who made the home. In the modern era, it is a partnership. Both the home-makers think, make decisions and carry them out to achieve a home which not only looks and feels good but exudes the very personal aura of its creators.

The in thing is not to yield blindly but to choose whatever appeals to you and then to go about planning it so that one can have different styles from different periods yet live in a fruitful co-existence of styles. Your house ends up being a reflection of your own individual personality.

Some Tips About Vaastu

Along with the revival of the Vaastu concept in Indian architecture, the West has been enthused by the ancient Chinese theory of design called Feng Shui which also stresses on certain architectural planning and aspecting so that the health and welfare of the inhabitants is ensured. A Vaastu perfect construction will have a positive bearing on the thinking, action and fate of people dwelling or working in these places and avoid disorderliness.

Has Vaastu something to do with architecture? Not really. While architecture is the science, art or profession of designing and constructing buildings etc. the definition of Vaastu extends into the realm of occultism.

Vaastu shastra, the edifice science of Bhawan Sthapatya Kala, being the applied aspects of Atharvaveda, is an ancient science and one of the eminent features of our heritage. Indeed, Vaastu is architecture and much more.

In Sanskrit literature, Vaastu means the dwelling of humans and gods. The universe is considered to consist of five elements, the earth, water, fire, air and space and the principles of Vaastu bring balance and harmony among these five elements leading to more flexibility of the body and mind of people enabling them to live a better life. Briefly, Vaastu can make the sweet things in life sweeter and the bitter less bitter. And, if construction is not according to the principles of Vaastu then thoughts and actions of the people dwelling or working in these places will not be harmonious and evolutionary, leading to disorderliness.

Building a house in ancient India was more than just a craft. It was a sacred ceremony where the house was considered a living organism, its spirit was called the Vaastu-Purusha and different cardinal directions and sectors were assigned to different Gods like Brahma, Ishwara, Agni, Varun, Vayu, and Yama. This was due to the belief that waves flowing in a particular direction have a specific influence. Eeshan or north east, for instance, is presided over by god, and is therefore suitable for a prayer room. The central space is Brahma's and should be left open to the Heavens while the head and limbs of the Vaastu. Purusha are to be left alone too. Scholars believe that various activities in a house, shop, office or industry, if directionally channelised as per principles of Vaastu, will begin to draw power from Nature. Once support from this force is forthcoming, all our objectives are fulfilled easily, effortlessly and spontaneously.

Vaastu shastra is being applied not only in the designing and construction houses but in commercial buildings and industries as well. For example, Vaastu assigns the kitchen, chimneys, furnace, boiler etc. to a certain corner on the basis of wind directions to prevent the smoke and cooking fumes from blowing into the living/working area and affecting the health of the residents/workers. This demands that architects and Vaastu engineers co-ordinate their activities. An architect can build a posh house but he cannot ensure a happy life to the people living in the house, whereas Vaastu science assures peace, prosperity and progress to the owner as also the inhabitants.

Many Vaastu rules appear common sense as they relate to ventilation and sunlight. But some like the subtle energy in natural and built environments that affect humans have also been verified and appreciated by those who did not believe in them initially. Here, the sun is the major cosmic entity which radiates light and heat. It is called self of the universe and so the principles of Vaastu allows human beings and society with inexhaustible source of energy and thus make them to live in a fully satisfied manner.

Along with its construction, the internal decoration in the house, shop or factory is equally important. If the settings of things are according to principles of Vaastu, the thoughts, speech and action are supported by nature and lead to health, wealth and happiness.

Vaastu current revival may be confined to human dwellings, but the scope of the shastra, also known as Sthapatya Veda extends to temple-design, isometry, town planning and civil engineering as well.

Most well known temples in South India like the Lord Venkateswara Temple at Tirupathi and the Meenakshi Temple at Maduri are Vaastu perfect. In terms of an entire city, Jaipur was founded in 1727 by Maharaja Sawai Jai Singh II in accordance with the principles of Vaastu shastra.

Vaastu do's and don'ts

Here are some tips and illustrations of the principles of Vaastu. The cardinal points are easily determined with the help of an ordinary compass.

- Plots with round, triangular, polygonal and other odd shapes may constantly lead one into some problem or the other. Square and rectangular plots are good. A family with a round or oblong dining table will suffer disharmony and end up not eating together.
- Blocking off the North-east (Eeshan) portion of the house/industry restricts the inflow of the blessings of God. It leads to tension, quarrel and insufficient growth of the inhabitants; especially the children.
- In an industry, any fault, ditch, broken part in the direction of North-east result in a handicapped child for the owner.
- Having improper position of the entrance/obstruction in front of the gate can reduce the prosperity.
- Improper position of the bed room or bed brings unhappiness in the married life. It also causes disturbed sleep.

- A water body or source should be in the east or north-east of the plot. Having a water body in the South-east/South portion of the house can cause damage to the male child or the wife of the owner. An underground water tank in the South-west can be fatal to the head of the family or the industry's owner.

- More open space in the north or east gives name, fame and prosperity. Leaving more space on the south-west side in the house can adversely affect the male members, whereas in industry it leads to financial loss and disputes amongst partners.

- Having a toilet/fireplace in the north-east corner of the house or industry can ruin it financially.

- A depression in the south-west can result in serious illness to the inhabitants whereas a depression in the north-west causes enmity and litigation. The depression in the south portion of the building restricts growth besides financial problems.

- Extension in the south-west may result in loss of health, money and other insurmountable problems whereas an extension in the south-east may lead to fire, accidents, theft and litigation.

- Heavy machinery has to be installed in the south-west in the factory.

- Finished products are to be kept in the north-west corner. It would help quick movement of the stocks and early recovery there off.

- Transformers, generators, motors, boilers, furnaces, oil engines etc. should be kept in the south-east or southern portion of the plot/ building.

- Central space is better left open or used for rituals. The traditional four-sided houses of Kerala and Rajasthan with a central courtyard and verandahs all around, is a model of Vaastu design.

- Although limited options are available to urbanites, benefits can accrue to the society if Vaastu guidelines are followed. An evenly planned construction of a house or a workplace following Vaastu principles is not possible, because of the levels in and around the plot, the plot's shape, the number of roads and their direction. Hence an architect or structural engineer has to work with the available plot and construct the house or the office to suit one's requirements under the given circumstances to provide maximum benefit to the inmates of the building.

- An architect or builder bestowed with the knowledge of Vaastu, designs the building striking a balance between the two and goes on benefiting society— thereby increasing his practice and acceptability manifold.

Colour

One of the first requisites demanded by everyone is satisfying colour schemes or even re-doing of a scheme which has palled or one which has been a disaster. Colour may be needed to brighten, to lighten a room or to counteract too high a ceiling, or to glamourize ordinary furniture.

Anyway, remember the old Cockney dictum popular in London? "A little bit of powder, a little bit of paint/ makes a girl pretty, even if she isn't!"

One finds in nature the seven colours of the rainbow transformed and transmuted into scores of colours to suit not only the room or the house but also your personality and individuality.

Colour, when correctly chosen and applied, can work miracles. It can make a too large room seem cosy, alternately give a sense of space to a too small one. It can brighten a too dark area and tone down the glare in another.

In short, colour is a highly evocative thing and for home-makers, it can prove to be the most inexpensive ingredient that creates a home to your taste. A home where you can live in comfort and which your friends love coming to.

You are all set for a happy home-making adventure, when you think of COLOUR.

Colour schemes fall basically into three groups: Monochrome, Related or Contrasting.

1. **Monochrome**: This scheme, as the name implies, features one basic colour in a variety of shades and textures.

   This colour scheme is beautifully set off with accents of contrasting bright colours in paintings, flower arrangements or dramatically coloured masks, lamp-bases, throw rugs, or the like.

2. **Related schemes**: These are made up of a combination of colours lying close together in the spectrum of the rainbow or the colour wheel. This is an exciting scheme for the person who has a titillating imagination. It can highlight the decor with one piece of sculpture or a painting.

3. **Contrasts**: These are relevant when the colours or their weights are widely different.

A working break-up to colour scheme

The factors which should be kept in mind while designing a colour scheme are the effect of adjacent colours each other and your own reaction to them.

The golden rule would be, avoid monotony and discord. The total effect should be a harmonious whole which is pleasing to the eye and senses.

Harmony is achieved by a combination of colours where they have something in common. This goes for both a Monochromatic or a Related scheme. For a contrasting scheme however, the apparent discord can be made harmonious by the use of one or more intermediate colours.

Adjacent colours and their effects

Colours influence each other by contrast when adjacent. A colour appears lighter when placed against darker shades.

Colours of the violet to green range, contain a high proportion of blue and appear cooler than the green-yellow to red-violet range, which have a high content of yellow. Green appears cool against a bright yellow but warm when surrounded by violet-blue. An interior has to stick to a natural tonal order. To reverse this is to create colour discord.

The Blacks, Greys and Whites: A cool elegance is achieved by grey walls, skirted at floor level with silver and black. They need a darker carpet. Black furniture set off by silver artifacts completes the picture.

Instead of silver and black braids, white and black ones, pale carpet and chrome furniture should be set off with judicious touches of red. A white wall, white furniture and a pale carpet look distinguished. Add touches of yellow and pink to stimulate the scheme.

The Browns, Beiges and Creams: These colours are easy to live with. Dark brown wall with a beige braid can adapt to any monochromatic scheme. The carpet is lighter and a rich effect is achieved by leather furniture. Brown wall with a darker brown braid calls for cream furniture, interspersed by colourful rugs and cushions.

Beige wall with white braid, a pale carpet and pale coloured furniture is made more delightful with accents of colour in accessories and pictures.

The Blues: Blue, repeated gloriously in sea and the limitless sky, is a moody colour and seems to change according to the way it is used. It can be dramatic when teamed with browns or greens and innocent and fresh when teamed with white. Deep blue wall, light blue and dark brown braids, deep blue carpet and light blue furniture is enlivened with touches of white in props. Use the same scheme with green furniture and touches of white, blue and pink in props. Light blue wall with white braid and dark blue carpet is charming with white furniture and green props.

Fabrics and drapes

Fabrics either mill-made or hand-woven are being manufactured in an endless variety of colour and design in the country.

When buying the fabric, one has to make sure that the colour is fast and that it will not shrink. The salesman will tell you if you want to wash and pre-shrink.

The next step is the hanging of curtains and drapes. Curtains can be hung either to the floor or to the window sill. Remember the hanging fabric is likely to stretch at the beginning, so tack the hem before hanging for the first time and allow a few days before doing the final stitching of the hem.

Methods of hanging curtains are basically two, the invisible track or the visible pole. There is quite a variety to choose from. The method of hanging will depend upon the weight of curtains. Tracks bear more weight easily and do not bend as is the wont of rods.

Curtains are expensive. It is more economical in the long run to line the curtains. Lining protects curtains from fading, when exposed to sunlight. Colours remain brighter and fresh longer.

In modern times curtains and drapes are no longer only adjuncts to privacy or against drafts or too bright sunlight, but very much a potent factor in modern decor.

The Window Treatment has to be studied, before you buy the material. On the visual side consider colour, texture, pattern to complement your colour scheme.

If you have a monochromatic scheme, you could have richly patterned curtains in beige, brown and cream in a room with a stark white interior, with a large window looking out at the front, think of a design with bold bright variegated colours which will look like stained glass with the light shining through it at night.

In a room with a related colour scheme, choose your curtains with an eye to complementing the most dominant colour.

A room with buttercup yellow walls in emulsion paint, natural sisal in curtain material looks well-matched. If your window looks out on a terrace, sheer curtains (sill length) will keep the garden view inside.

Alternately, a window with a depressing outlook would gain airy elegance with floor length sheer net curtains to camouflage the outlook.

In a room which gets too much sun, buy material that is not liable to fade. Big floral patterns or patterns with birds look delightful with the light shining through them. A better idea for children's rooms instead of the ubiquitous characters from comics. The same goes for brightly checked curtains and bedspreads.

With dramatic dark on dark and silver-white schemes, curtains and cushions can effectively repeat the pattern.

Small patterns look good in a room with much of waxed wood on floor and wainscoting.

Gingham, which is comparatively cheap, makes delightful curtains for not only the kitchen but for teenagers' rooms, with bedcovers and throw cushions repeating the colour. Finally, curtain material, be it silk, velvet, hand-weaves, or mill-made, should never be skimped. Enough fullness means elegance in curtains and drapes.

Light is essential

A well set up room done up in a colour scheme of your choice will lose its salient points if there is no proper lighting. A wrongly lit room falls flat.

Natural or artificial light affects colours, forms and textures, so in planning lighting attention needs to be given to both day and night aspects. Light—our friend. Away with the pendent bulb, hanging from the ceiling. Lights are there to serve for the specific purpose you need them and these needs are varied. For reading, for make-up purposes, for reading in bed, for cooking, for sewing, for television, for pictures and sculptures, even for cupboards and closets or those beloved indoor plants, there is the need for different kinds of lights.

Fortunately, the single bulb hanging from a flex has been replaced with a whole array of illuminating equipment in table lamps, standard lamps, picture lights, fluorescent lamps, spot lights, down lights. Your prized possessions, whether a picture, a piece of sculpture or a display can be highlighted to breathe new life into them, with spot lighting. Pictures should be down lighted for the maximum visual value. Lighting can correct the faults of a room, if it is too high, too low, too small or large. For instance an uplighter using a lamp placed on the floor against a wall makes the ceiling appear lower.

Functionally, correct placing of lighting is imperative in the work-areas, the kitchen, the study, the children's room and the dressing table.

Here is a simplified classification for your guidance:

a) General

b) **Directional/Two-directional:** This applies to two-way lighting on the stairs and the porch or hall for safety.

c) **Reflected:** This is particularly useful for relaxed reading. Diffused light reflected from a wall is devoid of glare yet bright for reading.

d) **Spot Lighting:** For getting the most value of your prized collections, sculptures or accessories.

e) **Down lighting:** Essential for the proper display of pictures.

f) **Decorative:** Optional lighting for special festivities.

The choice of lights should therefore depend upon functional aspect and the use of specific places in the house. Lighting is an important element in decor and requires careful planning.

Indoor plants

People had no need of the comfort and joy of indoor plants when urbanisation had not spread. Now it is a must. Foliage house plants need not be confined to the traditional philodendron and money plant. You have an endless assortment of sizes and shapes to choose from, plants of varied textured leaves and lovely hues.

It is best to have crotons, which will lend colour to your indoors or have arica palms, coleus, or exotic varieties like monstera, etc. inside your home.

Plant care

A house plant needs a clean pot, a loose-textured soil mixture and drainage materials such as clay shards of broken pots or large pebbles. Don't be worried if your plant loses a few leaves, because this is essentially a survival mechanism.

Allow the yellow scarred leaf to drop by itself, this way before following it will seal the point so that there is no wound to catch infections.

Watch your plant with loving care, which means adjust your watering to its needs. More house plants die of over-watering. Also sun it occasionally, it may droop with too dark a location.

Light is the power source by which leaves produce sugars and starches to feed all parts of a plant, so see that the plants get their vital food, light. Fortunately, tropical indoor plants need low light levels.

However, the light need of various houseplants vary according to their species. To summarize broadly, the crotons, coleuses and ivies require full sun or the bright reflected light bouncing off a light coloured wall.

The intermediate plants such as Begonias, Dracaenas thrive in partial, shade or light coming through a sheer curtain: Ferns survive in indirect shadowless light. If your plant is near a window, keep turning it to allow it to grow symmetrically.

What Decoration Achieves!

1. The magic of colour, and the effect of lights and lighting creates a mood and atmosphere in the house. It converts the brick and mortar walls into an aesthetic room.

2. Drapes, curtains, upholstery and carpets enhance the decor of your home, giving it an aura of plush comfort.

3. In decoration, the desired effect can be obtained with colour. A small room looks

large with light decorations while deep rich colours contract a large room.

4. A low ceiling will look higher if its in a lighter shade of the wall colour.

5. A room with poor light brightens up when the walls are papered with a cheerful sunny shade with a glossy surface.

6. A room into which strong sunlight pours in may be made subdued by decorating it in soothing shades such as blues and greens.

7. A narrow room will look broader if the ceiling and upper part of the walls are in a deeper shade than the lower portion. This sense of breadth is increased if the floor is covered with a plain carpet and the skirting painted in the same shade.

8. Adding a mirror to one wall of the room gives the illusion of depth.

The Importance of Having a Neat Entrance

In most houses and even smaller flats, there is either a spacious hall or even a small one which serves as the entrance to the house. Everyone from tradesmen to honoured guests enter the bungalow/flat from this entrance, hence it should be neatly maintained.

Both for reasons of security and for ventilation it is an asset to have a double door at the entrance so that one can see the person who wishes to enter. By having a mesh door through which one can see the person who wishes to enter, one can both regulate entry and simultaneously not jeopardise the security of the house by allowing unwanted salesmen or visitors to come in. In case there is no provision

for a double door, one would be well advised to have a keyhole or a chain on the door so that the visitor can be identified before granted access to the house.

Keys, umbrellas, raincoats row of untidy shoes on a shoe stand, children's bicycles, cricket bats, and rollers skates, as also school bags and shopping bags are frequently placed at the entrance for convenience.

However, it does not give an aesthetic appearance to visitors. Essentials should be neatly arranged or if they can be stored in a cupboard, that is the best solution to a neat entrance.

While a coir or rubber mat may be placed at the entrance to the house, there should be no loose rugs or small carpets at the entrance as when people are in a hurry these become a safety hazard as they slip.

The walls can be utilised to hang keys and if woollen coats or raincoats have to be kept, a cupboard should be made for this purpose. The walls should otherwise be aesthetically decorated with a suitable painting or statuette so that visitors get a good impression of the house owners.

Managing the exit

The back entrance of the house or flat which is frequently used by tradesmen, domestic help and children coming in from play, should also be neatly kept. Apart from having a mat on which dirty shoes may be wiped, the back entrance should also be organised so that empty crates, bottles, tins, cleaning equipment, and so on, do not clutter the exit. Things should be stored neatly so that they do not pose a hazard to those who are coming in or exiting the house from this point.

The Drawing Room or Living Room

The drawing room or living room is the main room of a house as it mirrors the personality of the owners. The decor of the drawing room, living room parlour or lounge reflects the tastes and interests of those living in the house. It is the one room in the house where outsiders have access as it serves as the centre of social activity. Good decor reflects the personality of the people who live in the home. Just as each person is distinctive, so too, the decor should be distinctive. It is not a mere question of expanse and expensive fittings, furniture and furnishings. Rather the entire room should be in harmony, not only with the furniture and furnishings in this room but also with the rest of the house. For example, if the living room is very small, then the furniture used

in it should be light so that the room does not look cluttered with outsized sofas and coffee tables. It is literally a question of cutting the cloth according to the coat, the furniture and the objets d'art should be placed or purchased only after ascertaining the size and style of the room.

There is nothing that makes a room or a single grouping of furniture look more inviting than the appearance for which it is used and enjoyed. To achieve this effect think of the activities that go on in the house and arrange groups or combinations of groups that will take care of all of them. For informal entertaining, chairs should be grouped in a way that two or more can sit easily together. For reading, there can be a lamp, a shelf for books and a place for magazines. A comfortable chair with a reading lamp can be kept for this purpose.

The drawing room should have upholstered furniture sufficient to seat all members of the family plus two to four guests. Each major chair should be within easy reach of a table having an ashtray and should be placed in a way that those entering the room can be seen and welcomed. Tables may contain lamps, books and other accessories both for utility and decoration. Table and chairs should harmonise in weight and style and seating furniture should be arranged either parallel or at right angles to the walls. Chairs and tables may also be placed diagonally whenever possible, units should be balanced with pieces of equal or similar design. Pairs of chairs, table, lamps help in this. The entire room should be linked together by means of something which is in common either by the colour of the wood, the style of the furniture, the colour scheme or some motif which blends the decor into one uniform whole. Even when there are different styles of furniture they should be placed in such a way that it matches with the rest of the pieces in the room.

Lighting

Apart from the natural light which streams into the room it is necessary to have artificial lighting that enhances the furniture and its accessories. There are ostentatious crystal chandeliers which are difficult to clean. There are recessed bulbs placed in the ceiling, standard lamps, table lamps, reading lamps and lamps to highlight a painting or a shelf of objets d'art. Although convenient in terms of the low wattage of electricity, it is advisable not to have tubelights or fluorescent lights in the drawing room as indirect lighting gives a better appearance to the room. The style of the lamps should match with the other decoration. The general lighting should be so designed that by switching them on or off the desired amount of lighting—bright, medium or dim can be achieved.

Floor or table lamps

These should be placed at focal points of interest to attract attention towards some picture hanging on the wall or a flower arrangement. Table lamps can be placed on tables, but if the table is low and only 22" from the floor, the lamps height including the shade should be 32". While high lamps look attractive with open tops so that light can be distributed, lamps that are below the eye level of a standing person should be covered from the top so that the bulb is concealed.

The appropriate material used for lamp shades are fabrics, handmade paper, raffia, reed and even metals and plastic.

Doing it up

Since the drawing room is a place where we entertain friends, it should be done up in pleasing colours with sturdy fabrics. After making a floor plan of the room, it is then safer to decide what to buy, what one already has and the budget for the room. The room should be planned by standing at the entrance as this is the view that all visitors will get on entering.

The drawing room has to be done up according to the needs and available space in the house. For those who have a special study or library, it may be more convenient to install the television and V.C.R, and books in that room. The stereo system, however, can be placed in the living room as gentle music in the background is always conducive to both relaxation and conversation. On the other hand, if the television is placed in the drawing room it may distract visitors and so compelling is its presence, that conversation ceases and all attention is focused on the T.V. screen. Books, while serving as an appropriate component of any living room, are also a source of distraction as visitors frequently get involved in browsing through the books. Sometimes a friend seeks to borrow a book, often it is not returned and then one gets into the unpleasantness of borrowing and securing the return of the book. If one has a library or study room, books and the television as also the computer are best placed in that room.

If lack of space necessitates placing of the television, V.C.R. and stereo system in the living room then it is best to have a wall unit in which these can be placed, along with a book area and a small bar. In selecting a built-in cabinet for the living room it is best to have shelves which are between 12" and 15" in depth.

The bar must be at least 1 ft. high so that large bottles can fit in. There should be a shelf for glasses as well, preferably with a rim, so that they do not slip out.

Upholstered furniture

When buying upholstered furniture, certain features should be carefully checked. Firstly it should be comfortable to sit on and should be the right height to sit on. The cost of this furniture depends on its inner construction. Two identical pieces of upholstered furniture are sometimes entirely different in quality and cost. Upholstered furniture consists of five parts—frame, seat, springs, fillings and fabric.

The upholstery fabric should be bought carefully not only because it is expensive but also because the entire impact of the room depends on it. Fabrics cover a considerable area so they have to be selected on the basis of their texture, colour, pattern and expense. While upholstery fabric and draperies reflect the taste of those who buy them, a simple rule to follow is that if there is a great deal of patterned upholstery, the drapes should be plain and vice versa so that there are no clashing patterns all around. Light coloured upholstery fabrics give an airy and spacious look but light colours are difficult to maintain, especially with houses where there are small children. Earthy colours suggest the outdoors, while dark colours and small patterns give a cosy appearance.

While some people are able to change their furnishings frequently, for those who are unable to, it is best to select durable, natural coloured fabrics for both drapes and upholstery.

Slip covers or chairs which require just a cushion, the rest being wood work can be changed more frequently and also washed or dry cleaned. Different sets of cushion covers can be made for winter and summer so that the living room gets a new look depending on the season.

To obtain a cool look for summer, heavy rugs should be removed and replaced by durries, reed matting or smaller throw rugs. Heavy winter draperies can be replaced with light summer drapes. Slip covers in soothing colours, such as green, blue and white should cover upholstered furniture, both as a summer change as well as to give protection against dust and fading.

Carpets

Whether antique Persian rugs, handwoven Kashmiri carpets, machine-made carpets, durries or jute matting, some form of carpeting is necessary in a living room as it lends a complete, finished look to the room.

A few benefits of carpets are that they absorb noise, make the floor and protect a person from falling down the stairs. The most important impact of a carpet is that it creates an impression of luxury and establishes the colour scheme in a room.

Whereas wall-to-wall carpeting is a necessity in foreign countries to keep out the bitter cold, in India it is not strictly required especially in residential accommodation. Rugs are more easily handled and easier to clean. They can be shifted from room to room and also house to house during transfers.

Whereas wall-to-wall carpeting gives an illusion that the room is larger, covers irregularities in the floor and creates a feeling of luxury, warmth and quiet as it diffuses noise made by footsteps, it is nevertheless difficult to clean and maintain, subject to stains, especially in a house in which there are small children.

A **rug** is a single piece floor covering made with a pattern and which has a border with a fringe.

A **room-sized rug** is one that covers within 12 inches or less from the walls on all sides.

An **area rug** is one which is placed in a large room to demarcate a certain area.

A **scatter rug** is a small rug that is used to complement the decor in a room and is placed in front of the bed or dressing table etc.

An **accent rug** is placed on a wall-to-wall carpet, which is usually plain, to give some colour and complement the colour scheme in a room.

For low budgets felt, jute, coir, cotton or even *chatais* are available to enhance the decor of the room. An advantage of area rugs or scatter rugs is that furniture can be placed around it, rather than on it. When heavy furniture is placed on the carpet it causes a certain amount of wear and tear on it, hence the furniture should be shifted around periodically and the carpet brushed so that it does not get damaged.

Objets d'art in the living room—paintings, sculpture, porcelain and crystal are some of the accessories that are placed in the drawing room. Although tastes differ from person to person, it may be noted that calendars, children's toys, plastic decorations and flowers do not constitute appropriate decoration for living room as these give a tacky appearance to the room. While expensive accessories are not essential, and nor is it necessary to have the room resemble a museum or art gallery, the choice of objects to be kept in the living room should be aesthetic and appropriate. For example, paintings of nude women, sculptures showing an exaggeratedly voluptuous female form are also not in good taste for the drawing room. The right accessories not only enhance the appearance of the room but also reflect the good taste and artistic sensibilities of the owner. The objets d'art and paintings should blend in with and enhance the decor and overall colour scheme of the room.

To avoid clutter, one can rotate the accessories if one has too many so that the visitors are always treated to something new when they come in. The living room accessories can be rotated according to the season with warm-coloured lamps and dark oil paintings for the winter, gay fragile vases and vivid water colours for the spring and crystal flower containers and figurines in white porcelain for the summer.

While accessories lend character and reflect the personality of the owner, too many homes get cluttered after years of random accumulation. Periodical removal of unnecessary objects is wise.

Delicate porcelain, crystal and other fragile items may be placed in a glass covered cabinet or wall shelves with glasses so that they are protected from both dust and damage.

The Dining Room or Dining Area

Whereas some houses may have a separate dining room, which is ideal, others may have a combined drawing-cum-dining room. The dining area or dining room has special decoration requirement from that of the drawing room. Whereas the drawing room is used to entertain visitors the dining room is constantly used by members of the family several times a day. In a house where there are small children there is a constant danger of food spill on the floor, therefore, it is best to keep this area free from carpeting. Even scatter rugs are a hazard as the housewife or servant may slip on it while rushing in and out with the food.

The furniture and decor must be adapted to the size, lighting, proximity to the living room and the amount and type of entertaining contemplated. Expandible tables are available in drop-leaf, extension console or dining room types in which leaves are inserted. Folding chairs may be stored so that the problem of crowding too many chairs into a limited space is eliminated.

If the dining area is connected with the living room, the decor and the rug should blend with it.

Placement of furniture

While the dining table is generally placed in the centre of the room with dining chairs all around it, if the room is very small, there is provision for a folding dining table that would require just 120 cm ∞ 80 cm of spare wall area. The table would seat five people and it can be fixed to the wall with four screws and pulled out whenever required. It becomes a decorative wall piece when not in use.

Dining tables can be wooden, wooden with sunmica top, cane with glass top and a wooden base and marble top table. If there are children in the house it is best to ensure that the table has rounded rather than sharp edges so that it is not a hazard to the child. A marble top table is easy to keep clean and is also durable, though not so easily transportable.

Side boards

Side boards can be used on one side of the wall to keep cutlery and crockery. Alternatively, if there is a wall unit then glasses, plates and decorative items may be placed in them. One drawer can be kept to store placements and other table linen. The top of the side board may be decorated with candle stands, flowers, decanters, silver fruit stands and other appropriate bric-a-brac. Additional storage space may be provided by a corner cupboard. The bar is frequently kept in the dining room. A tea-wagon or tea-trolley placed in the dining room serves as a great serving aid.

Table settings

Table settings will be discussed at length in a later chapter. For daily meals there may be table cloths or table mats. In homes where there are small children it may be more practical to have table mats as a table cloth may frequently be tugged by the child leading to a dangerous situation in which glasses and plates may fall to the floor causing injury and damage.

Table mats are available in all shapes, sizes and materials. Many use plastic mats as these are easy to maintain and, therefore, convenient for daily use. However, when guests come, table mats give a better appearance. Mats can be made of cloth, jute, bamboo and can be purchased to match with the colour of the crockery.

Table decoration

In those dining rooms where the table is placed at the centre, may be decorated with a flower vase placed at the centre. For parties, silver candle stands or porcelain candle stands may be placed on either side of a central floral piece. Small porcelain/pottery animal figures may be placed around this floral centre piece. Alternatively a fruit stand with fruits can form a central decoration piece for change on a daily basis.

The Bed Room

A bed room constitutes possibly the most important element of a house. It is around this space that members of the family unwind

after a hard day's work. It serves as a retreat and refuge from the outside world, a room in which one can really be oneself. There are no do's and don't in a bedroom and one can decorate it in any way that one feels like. Comfort and convenience for the user is the chief buzz word for this room.

The main pieces of furniture in a bedroom are, of course, a bed, a side table, cupboards, a dressing table, chairs to enable a seating arrangement, a writing desk and possibly a television and stereo system.

While the bed may simply be of wood, it may also include a frame, headboard, four posts (especially if mosquito nets are to be used), or even a canopy. Some bedrooms have no bed but consist of some thick mattresses placed on the floor. Others have elaborate headboards made of wood and are plain, carved, painted, or even upholstered. The headboard sets the style of the room and may be done in leather, satin, chintz, silk, gingham or rough handlooms. Some headboards have built-in book shelves and a lighting system to facilitate bed time reading.

Dressing tables may be simple or elaborate, with three way mirrors and drawers to keep one's cosmetics and other things such as combs, hairbands, lipsticks and so on.

A full-length mirror on the closet or entrance door facilitates dressing. Lighting in a bedroom should be provided according to one's requirements. There could be some general lighting and then reading lights, lights over the dressing table and at the desk. While floor rugs can be colourful, they should harmonize with the curtains which may be of silk, organdy, handloom or printed floral cottons. The bedspreads add colour and character to the room.

Paintings, posters and a desk calendar where one enters the engagements for the day are useful in the bedroom. Also, an extension of the telephone, along with on address book are often needed in the bedroom.

A seating arrangement with a table can be laid alone the bed and stacked with current newspapers and magazines.

Many beds have built-in storage space which is useful for putting away extra pillows and mattresses. Mattresses and pillows must be chosen with considerable care as a mattress which is not comfortable viz., either too soft or too hard will give rise to back aches. The same is true of pillows. Some people are allergic to the cotton in pillows so they should choose the new ones made of non-allergic foam.

While the earlier trend was to have plain white bed sheets and pillow cases, still followed in five star hotels, floral prints are very attractive and are less likely to show stains and dirt. There is no limit to one's imagination in doing up one's bedroom so that it is both aesthetic, functional and yet a reflection of one's own needs and personality.

Wall cupboards or steel cupboards are essential to keep one's clothes safely and in an organised manner. Some houses have built-in wooden closets in which one portion is made of steel with a safe so that valuables can be kept in them. For men's clothes especially, a cupboard with provision for hanging clothes is essential. Sarees and salwar kameezes may also be hung. The other method is to fold sarees and keep them in neat rows, with blouses and petticoats kept in separate piles. As far as possible, shoes should not be kept in the same cupboard as the clothes, but there can be either a separate shoe cupboard or provision for shoes to be kept under the cupboard.

The Children's Room

Here the colour scheme should be strong and simple and furniture sturdy, accident proof and easy to keep clean. There should be ample provision for keeping toys and books and walls should be painted with washable paint. Paintings can be bright wooden cutouts of cartoon characters and animals can be used. Pictorial charts and maps may be of interest to the child. A large bulletin-board would enable the child to put up interesting pictures and messages.

Rugs in a child's room should be made of easily washable material. Furniture should include a junior bed with removable side rails if necessary. Alternatively there can be a full-sized bed with a firm mattress, a chip proof or inexpensive table and one to three chairs, a clothes chest, closet and desk for the school-going child. A fundamental rule in furnishing a child's bedroom is that children grow quickly and their needs change from year to year. Too many pieces of miniature furniture may be a waste in the long run. In a nursery, the child's cot constitutes the central piece of furniture. A chest of drawers to hold the child's clothes and toys and an easy chair/rocking chair for the mother are required. The furniture and curtains in the nursery can be in gay colours.

As the child grows he can use a bigger bed and toys should be kept within easy reach so that he can keep himself amused. If siblings share a room, bunker beds which are double decker beds are real space savers.

School children will require a study table, a reading lamp and book shelves.

Teenagers have their own ideas about room decoration and may favour posters and pin-ups of their favourite film or sport stars. One should avoid confrontation with the teenager on this subject and can give in to their whims and fancies as long as their suggestions are not outrageous in terms of taste and propriety.

When two siblings share the room there may be a lot of conflict and irritations but there is no better way of preparing the child for the future than by encouraging him or her to share.

The Guest Room

The guest room which used to be an intrinsic feature of all big houses is increasingly rare in small apartment. Hence, it can be a dual purpose room which can be put to use throughout the year. The purpose of the room is to make the guest feel welcome and comfortable. It enables both the guest and the host to maintain privacy.

Furniture for this room should be selected with due care. A sofa-cum-bed is a viable alternative than having two beds. There should be a bedside table with a lamp and if possible a table for suitcases. If there is a built-in cupboard, provision should be made for the

guests to hang their clothes. A mirror fitted over a desk should have some letter papers, a pen, a candle stand with candle and matches in case of a power cut and a few magazines.

The guest room may have two easy chairs so that the guest feels a gracious welcome.

The drapes, bedspreads and rugs can be in some pleasing colours. A waste paper basket must be placed in the room.

The Study

The study should cater to intellectual requirements of the family members. It should balance the dual needs of relaxation and mental stimulation.

The main pieces of furniture should be:

- a desk
- a straight back chair
- a wall shelving unit
- a diwan

The wall shelving unit may be used for audio-visual equipment such as the television,

V.C.R, music system and so on.

The computer may be placed either on the desk or on a separate table. Space for other electronic equipment such as a fax machine can also be provided for.

It is important to pay attention to the electrical connections while installing these so that there are no safety hazards. The wiring should be insulated and placed along the walls so that room looks neat and chances of getting shocks are negligible. If required one should take the assistance of an electrician to install the gadgets correctly.

Bean bags can also be placed to provide seating.

The wall shelving unit should have provision for keeping books, photo-albums, audio and video cassettes and CDs which should preferably be kept covered so as not to collect dust. This unit could either:

- be kept open;
- have sliding glass panes; or
- wooden doors.

Lists of audio-video cassettes, CDs and computer floppies should be made either:

- subject wise; or
- in an alphabetical order.

The walls may either have paintings or family photographs. The floor may be carpeted or have scattered rugs.

A diwan if placed in this room should have colourful cushions and could serve as an extra bed in case of guests.

The Utility Room or Store Room

In earlier houses, every kitchen had a store room. In this room extra rations such as rice, sugar, pulses, etc. were kept. Today not all houses have a store room attached to the kitchen due to lack of space. Kitchen cabinets however are a substitute to the store room. However some houses do have a utility room which can be used for ironing clothes, keeping extra suitcases, extra bedding, children's bicycles and so on.

The rule here is that there should be a place for everything in the house and everything should be in its place, therefore, the store room must be de-gunned at regular intervals. Old newspapers, bottles, shoes, clothing, books etc. must be collected and sold off periodically to the "kabadiwala."

Storage Ideas

Making every inch work

Ingenious storage ideas to make good use of nooks and crannies requires imagination and planning.

With accomodation problems on the rise and more and more people living in cramped apartments, space is at a premium today. Gone are the days of large storage rooms lined with steel trunks and pickle jars. In this world of compact living, even a separate store seems to be an unaffordable luxury. Yet, to use a given space to the maximum advantage, all that we need are a few space saving tips and a bit of effective planning.

1. Wall area, an often neglected space, can be used to create ample storage in the form of shelving.
2. Fold out table tops can extend work surfaces.
3. The dead space below staircases is used effectively with a two-tier storage system.

The bedroom

Apart from built-in cupboards covering an entire wall area and loft, extra storage can be created in the form of drawer units under the bed or an entire storage box with a cushioned lid for seating can be supported on castors.

1. In the children's room, bunker beds use up the floor area of one bed to accomodate two.
2. Shelves and even fold out writing desks could be incorporated along with toy display units and drawers for the usual knick-knacks.

3. Book shelves, too, could find a place in the unit while hollow cubes form a storage unit with the option of adding

up the units in different permutations and colours to add variety. The entire shelving unit in the children's room could be painted over in bright colours with games, cartoons and fairy tale characters stuck on to make an interesting feature.

4. Another space saving device in the kid's room is having two beds of unequal height with one bed on rollers sliding under the other during the day time. During study hours, writing desks could be folded out of the wall shelving unit to use up the empty space.

Bathroom

1. Apart from cabinets below the wash-basin counter, storage space can be created in a number of ways inside the toilet. Because most bathrooms are small to begin with, the storage problems are magnified but with simple additions in the toilet, one could go a long way.

2. Check the unused wall space available. Even the wall area behind the water closet, which we generally give up on, can be used to provide much needed storage space. The entire wall area behind the toilet seat could be converted into a shelving unit with the w.c. itself fitting into a larger size open shelf. Extra rolls of toilet paper, towels and medicines could be stocked here, along with reading material. For those in the habit of reading in the loo, the shelving unit could be converted into a veritable library.

3. Another usable area is the wall above the wash-basin. A dressing cabinet to store cosmetics and medicines with a mirror fixed on to the shutter could be very helpful.

Similar ideas could work wonders in the laundry room.

Not only do they help keep the laundry room tidy, they can also speed up the work and make washing a pleasant job.

1. A shelving unit-cum-hanger rod suspended from the ceiling helps save floor space and provides a unit for hanging up clothes to dry.

2. It could also stock detergents and scrubbing brushes.

3. A wall shelving system could fold out to form an ironing board with an inbuilt plug for the iron. A soft board mounted on one of the shutters could make an innovative tackboard for pinning up messages, monthly planners and important notes.

4. Within the laundry room, a double wardrobe system helps store clothes which are not in season. With one stationary component acting as a cupboard, the other swings in to create a shutter, providing double the storage.

Within the house, effective storage areas could come in the form of wall partitions. Used as visual room dividers and also useful in drawing-cum-dining area, the entire full height partition could be made of shelves for displaying curio pieces. A still more flexible room divider is one which can be taken apart completely and reassembled at a fast pace. Cutting a few notches and grooves into the planks helps the members fit in together to form a wall shelf or room divider as the situation demands.

In rooms with high ceilings, a mezzanine loft can be added to increase the usable floor space. The space below the staircase can be used to stock books in open shelves or just about any extra item through a method of pull out shelving compartment, sliding on rollers.

Inside the kitchen, similar space saving options could come in the form of swing out double shelving units and cabinet shutters opening out to form hinged informal dining tables. When not in use, the table can be folder back and the floor space saved. Magnets help display messages and recipes on the refrigerator door and adding semi-circular shelves to the door of an existing corner cabinet could turn a dead end space into an easy to reach usable area.

Use a counter space for keeping all electrical gadgets like mixers, grinders etc. and provide plug points and overhead cabinets to store the appliances when not in use. Wall mounted shelves could store utensils, condiments and also a few recipe books. Another welcome addition could be a pullout shelving unit on castors to serve as a serving trolley when needed or tucked safely inside a cabinet.

All these units can be made out of 3/4" block board finished with teak lipping and laminated or duco painted to give a sleek look. For areas not prone to heavy usage, fabric could be clad over the board to add an interesting texture in bedrooms and living areas with colours selected to match the upholstery.

In order to economize on space, it is better to use sliding instead of swing out shutters for cabinets as well as doors. Adjustable sizes of shelves too make the entire storage system more effective.

■■

CHAPTER-5

Making a Home Happy!

Be Happy, Be Positive

The four walls, adorned with costly paintings, valuable rugs on marble floor and expensive crockery and cutlery do not necessarily constitute a happy home. A happy home consists of happy family members who have adopted, cultivated or are imbued with certain correct attitudes which contribute towards making theirs a happy home. In the ultimate analysis, happiness is a question of perception and one can always see a cup as being either half full or half empty. When travelling abroad, one is often asked how it is that Indians are always smiling and talking even though they are either very poor or atleast surrounded by poverty. All the material goods and individual liberty have not made westerners a happy lot.

Traditional Indians are happy with their position in life, because of the philosophy of Karma which is based on the belief that one's deed's in a past life influence the present. Hence one has to work hard so that one does better in the next life and in the meanwhile one must accept and make the best of what one gets. Joys and sorrows, good health and illness, success and failure are all part of this cosmic reality.

Modern thinking, particularly in Europe and America, places a lot of emphasis on the individual, his effort and his hardwork. Not much emphasis is placed on the elements of luck, chance or fete and no quarter is given to the possibility of failure. Hence when things don't go their way, as they planned or worked for it, they get depressed, pressured, anxious and require 'counselling' so that they may come to terms with it. Too much emphasis is placed on success and material prosperity and individual self-worth is linked to the trappings of either power, success or riches. With increasing consumerism and an admiration for Western values, people in India, particularly in the corporate sector where there is a great emphasis on targets and their achievements, people are beginning to suffer the same syndrome of performance, success, targets and also unhappiness, depression, stress, anxiety, panic attacks and low self-esteem. This is quite at variance with our traditional values in which the man of spirituality and learning was placed at the top of the hierarchy, the man of action or the warrior was placed next and the man of business placed only third. It is only with Westernisation that mammon worship has caught on and the abbreviations that have crept in with it, would now to put any Westerner to shame.

The problems of success and plenty may have appeased a material hunger in the west but it has brought in it's wake a realization that there is a great emptiness in their life. Individual quest and success has increased selfishness and has alienated him from the family system. Rushing from one transient relationship to another has only increased their insecurity but they are now too used to the impermanence and freedom that such relationships offer. Hence, unhappy people flit from one person to the other causing themselves more trauma and low self-esteem.

You can achieve whatever you think you can as consciously and unconsciously you will work towards your mission. Life is full of obstacles, failures and bad health and no one is free of this. The only difference between those who succeed and those who don't is that the positive individual knows how to cope with the hurdles and accepts them as part of life enabling him to cope with adversity and coming out stronger.

Never get tripped or fazed by the problems that come your way. Take it as a challenge to prove yourself and adopt the resilience of a bouncing ball. Negative thoughts and negative thinking do not help in any way but only make things worse. Also remember that every problem is transient and recall the old adage 'This too will pass.' Depression arises when one feels that one is helpless and that the situation in which things are going wrong will last forever. It happens with everyone but can be tackled if one says 'that I am emotionally drained and need to take better care of myself

and rest so that I can feel good tomorrow this'. If one thinks in manner the depression will ease and disappear.

Negative thinking breeds depression and is contagious. If one is living with someone who is gloomy and critical, it is contagious as one gets depressed not only by being around such a person but also because one gets depressed thinking about the other's unhappiness. Moreover, negative thinking kills the present and the future because of thinking that the worst may happen. Better to think that nothing bad will happen!

Tips on Positive Thinking

1. If you are feeling negative do something to change your mood by going into a new environment, by visiting a friend, going shopping or going to a cinema or play.

2. Do things that make you happy—watch TV, read a book or go for a walk.

3. While neither the past nor the future can be changed. C, change the present by having a positive approach.

4. Get some exercise as exercise releases certain chemicals that are mood elevators and which destroy tension. Even cleaning out cupboards is fine.

5. Rest, sleep and relaxation afford a respite from fatigue that in turn encourage positive thoughts.

6. Refuse to think negatively when things don't go your way so that you avoid self-pity. Never say
   > I have no will power.
   > I did a bad job.
   > I look terrible.
   > I hate myself.

7. Concentrate on your achievements rather than your drawbacks.

8. Believe in your successes and your accomplishments and give a boost to your self-esteem.

Laughter Banishes the Blues

The proliferation of laughing clubs in our cities goes a long way in proving that laughing has now become a serious matter. One may notice that as one grows older one laughs less and this in turn increases one's stresses and strains. A hearty laugh not only dispels gloom but acts as an antidote to depression and enhances good health.

In many ways laughter seems to have gone with the joint family. Today, even children do not laugh as much as they should, burdened as they are with unwieldy courses, early competition and the constant pressure to excel. Said one dour parent, 'It's a question of laughter versus starving! We have no time for laughter anymore. It has to be hard work. I have worked every minute of my life to see that my children succeed.' Little wonder that heart attacks, diabetes, stress, anxiety and depression are rising steadily.

Thus laughter clubs have come up and January 10 is celebrated as world laughter day. The endeavour of its members is to remind the world that human beings are the only species blessed by the Almighty to laugh.

Laughter has been synonymous with the sound of happiness, a touch of joy and the wisdom of ages enjoins that it is the best medicine for healthy and harmonious living. Laughter is said to have a powerful healing effect on many diseases and women rate a good sense of humour as one of the important attributes in a man.

A healthy laugh is said to trigger off life—enhancing hormones that are so powerful that a person's entire immune system can help it to ward off diseases even helping to fight cancer.

A professor of psychoneural immunology at the New York State University, who has been a pioneer in laughter research has provided the most conclusive evidence yet of a link between laughter and immunoglobin A, an antibody which helps fight illness by marking out harmful invading bacteria and viruses. Another vital chemical triggered by laughter is cytokines, dubbed the 'happy hormone' which promotes the activity of white blood cells which specialise in fighting off invading bacteria and viruses and destroy potential tumour cells.

It is an unequal world and life is often unfair. We cannot always get what we want, but that does not mean we cannot be happy. There is no better way than to laugh our way to happiness and by facing our adversities with a smile.

What better way to heal a person than to make him laugh since laughter is the best medicine?

Laughter is one of the best medicines in tackling lifestyle diseases such as stress, high blood pressure, depression, psychological problems and even heart disease. All these troubles arise out of the modern syndrome of taking oneself and one's problems too seriously. Some specialists have equated laughter with meditation—you not only lose track of time but you emerge a more relaxed and carefree person later on.

The best form of humour is the ability to laugh at yourself and your own mistakes, and to make light of your personal problems.

So, if you thought humour was a funny business, think again. There is nothing more exhilarating in life than having the last laugh. Don't take laughter for granted but cultivate it as the great tension releaser and dispeller of gloom and doom.

Never consider laughter as frivolous and unbecoming as many serious minded peopled appreciate laughter and use it to win friends.

Adjustment is Necessary

'Adjustment is necessary' insisted our mother and to make any relationship work and to achieve success one must adjust to the situation, to different circumstances, different environments and different people.

Today the theme is 'I', ' Me', 'My'—everyone believes that he or she is the centre of the universe and that the world and everyone in it should function according to what we want and expect. The western concept of stressing on the individual has percolated down to us also and the women's lib movement in particular has emphasized that the onus of adjustment has always been on the woman and she has thus lost her individuality. This is a concept for theoreticians but in real life one will notice that everyone has to adjust and they have—be it men to women, husband to wife, parents to

children, children to parents, daughters in law to mothers in law and sons in law to fathers in law.

The spirit of adjustment and accommodation must be inherent and cultivated so that living and working with others becomes easy. In many ways, the ego is inborn and we many tend to put ourselves above all else. However, this instinct has to be kept in check so that we can live and function with others in society as well as in personal relationships. We should promote mutual harmony'. Harmony and adjustment are virtually two sides of the same coin. We have to take into consideration another person's needs, habits, temperament and mould ourselves to accommodate the other person.

In a marriage situation for example, two people are required to live together and share everything from morning till night—one bed, one bathroom and one house has to be shared. Therefore, we must adjust or modify some of our habits and needs to harmonise with our partner. Why is it that many marriages crumble even after a couple has known each other for a long time? This is often because when called upon to spend 24 hours together under the same roof, each person may find the habits of the other intolerable!

The concept of sharing of putting others before yourself, sometimes if not always, must be taught to our children and must be practiced by us. By adjusting with others we do not become lesser individuals, rather we become supreme and superior, managing in every situation and with every type of person and their individual idiosyncrasies.

Patience is a Virtue

In a life of instant, the fact that patience is a virtue is no longer reiterated. However, we need to remember that patience is a fruit of the spirit just as love is. Patience does not mean inactivity—it means that people are to go on with their work and duty without necessarily getting their instant rewards. In a world of desperate and irrational haste, patience is the art of pacing.

The beauty of patience is that it helps to still a restless mind in its haste to seek appreciation, gain success, reap rewards and achieve goals. The world does not move as we want it to and hence we must steel ourselves to be patient and inculcate in our children the notion that instant gratification is not always possible. If a person has not learnt to be patient, he has learnt very little.

Tidiness is a Must

Although our burgeoning population has not yet forced us to live in tiny spaces as in Tokyo, dwellings are no longer as spacious as what they used to be. Our cities in particular, which have increased in size and numbers, now boast of huge populations which have to be accommodated within a limited space. Flats and houses are getting smaller and space is really at a premium. In Tokyo, people live in miniscule flats and visitors have to check into 'capsule' hotels in which most of the furniture folds into the wall or projects from it at a height. At the same time, the demands of a materialistic and consumerist society are such that we are buying and accumulating more than what we can use. Along with this comes a frenetic pace of life in which we are always rushing in and out of the house on errands, work or social obligations. More than ever before it is essential for us to be tidy as too many people in too small a place with too many things leads to untidiness. The need therefore is to have a space for everything and everything in its place.

No matter how busy one is or how tired, tidiness has to be maintained, particularly in small apartments where every room is on display and where neatness is an essential prerequisite. The easiest way to be tidy is:

1. To have a place for shoes, newspapers, clothes and toys. All family members should cooperate in keeping the place tidy by putting things back in their right place.

2. Once there is a place for everything then putting things back where they belong is a matter of ten minutes everyday, whenever one has the time.

3. Children should be encouraged to put their clothes, shoes and toys back in their appointed place.

4. No matter how beautiful the decor and how costly the furnishings, neatness has its own beauty and an untidy room is an eyesore. Therefore ensure that beds are made, that bedcovers and carpets are not crooked, that curtains are properly pulled and cushions are plumped into shape. Tidiness enhances the decor.

5. If your house is enough or if there is a corner of your room which can accommodate a chair, place your 'extras' on it and put it away as soon as you have time in their appointed place in your cupboards.

6. Tidiness also ensures order and eliminates time that is wasted in looking for things amidst clutter.

Anger—A Volatile Emotion

While some believe that to discharge one's feelings is beneficial, and that people should hit out when frustrated, others are of the view that uncontrolled expression of anger is detrimental to health. Anger is one of the most awesome emotion felt by a human being, yet one which can cause widespread disturbance—both in an individual and where collective anger is involved such as in strikes and riots, looting and arson—to society in general. This primeval emotion has been responsible for wars and persecution of racial groups such as Hitler against the Jews, or whites against blacks in South Africa, and in the US. Anger may be thought of as a great motivating emotion, as it can spur on an individual to prove oneself in an endeavour to combat past humiliation, hurt, insult or man-made impediments in one's path towards a particular goal. One may cite the examples of those individuals who have undertaken the cause of the downtrodden, or women leaders who have taken up the fight against the torture and humiliation of women in this country. It was the emotion of anger against the treatment meted out to individuals or group causes which have spurred them on.

There are certain physical accompaniments to anger. When aroused, the pituitary glands release a hormone called adrenaline which fills the blood stream and ignites the chemistry of the human system. As a result, every sinew, nerve and muscle is filled with a sort of super power which instantly endows us with a strength which is beyond our normal capacity.

Certain people are always raging about something - from being held up in traffic to waiting in queues. They shout and rant and blame others when things go wrong. Constant hostility of this type leads to high blood pressure, which again is linked to coronary heart diseases and strokes. Such personality types are frequently able to channelise their anger into political movements, social work or business, frequently rising high in the organisation due to their heightened competitiveness. However, those around them who are less vocal or powerful may have to bear the fruit of their anger, such as subordinates, spouses, servants and children. This presents a no-win situation as repressed anger can lead to depression, arthritis, asthma, blood pressure and ultimately heart trouble. If negative feelings are expressed as they are experienced, there is no destructive rage, since feelings are not bottled up.

The ability to express anger has much to do with preconditioning during one's childhood. A small child who is constantly nagged by the mother, severely punished for throwing tantrums or rebuked by an older sibling is more likely to develop into an easily angered adult. Suppressed anger can lead to suicide, depression and violent behaviour ranging from physical violence and drug taking, to murder.

A growing child or a teenager has to cope with emotions as well as frustration in various spheres of life as part of the growing up process. Careful guidance and an abundance of love from parents, especially the mother will go a long way towards helping the child to cope with feelings of anger and aggression. With maturity some measure of control comes in. Hence, Yogic meditation is highly beneficial as it helps to still the mind and bring mental peace. It also encourages reflection which is essential for every adult, as the fast pace of modern life leaves no time to ponder over, or analyse one's drawbacks, ambitions, frustrations and goals. Reflection and self-analysis is essential to cope with anger.

Dealing with Anger: It has to be understood that like joy and sorrow, anger too is a natural emotion and should be dealt with as such. One must remember that it is possible to love and hate somebody at the same time. So one need not feel guilty about being angry with them. One should go straight to the cause of one's anger without misdirecting it into distant objects or those who are powerless. Encourage children to talk about their hurts and resentments so that they become communicators rather than suppressed individuals. Most of all self-control, reflections and self-analysis must be done to analyse the cause of one's anger. By this method we can make anger work for us in a positive way and hence it can spur us on to positive improvements rather than negative destruction. With a bit of self-restraint, we could look back on anger as something we have conquered rather than the reverse. It should be remembered that over the centuries angry men and women have maimed and murdered, destroyed cities and exterminated civilizations. In an increasingly violent society it is imperative that we understand and control this emotion.

The Power of Love

A new field of research called psychoneuro-immunology (PNI) reveals a link between the brain and the immune system. Laboratory tests have revealed that married women had stronger immune systems and that happily married women had the strongest immune system of all. Studies with men produced similar results. Contact and warm personal relationship with others contributed to health and longevity. Today, western research is corroborating what our forefathers already emphasized when they stressed that the mind and body were closely connected. Homeopathy and Ayurveda take into consideration the mental and emotional state of a person when treating illness.

It is the power of love that enables children to grow. An experiment was conducted on babies who were fed and then cuddled by their mothers. Another group of babies were fed and then put back into their cradles without either being cuddled or held closely. The growth in the babies who were cuddled was much faster than those who were merely cleaned, fed and put into their cots. Can love, that ephemeral thing of the mind, contribute to our physical well-being. All religions, most singers and many poets have long since waxed eloquent about the power of love.

The mandate to love your neighbour as yourself is not just moral but also physiological.

Love, caring and closeness have the potential of being stress relievers as those who are loved feel less alone, less threatened and more confident of facing stress because they know they have someone to turn to. The feelings of security, optimism and hope are great antidotes to success. Holding close, hugging, snuggling, petting, stroking, touching—is all good for your health, your heart and of course, your relationships.'

Unconditional love is the medicine for today's stress and tension burdened society. Love is soothing, physically, mentally and emotionally and the lack of it can make us physically sick, create emotional imbalance and disharmony. Adults too need love as nourishment as much as children and elders too need to be loved and felt loved so that they do not fall into the degenerate diseases of the aged.

Nobody can live wholly in his job. Although too many workaholics are trying to do, thinking that they can dispense with intimate relationships and get along with the casual personal contacts of the job and the club. It would be better if we acknowledged our need for love and affection and then tried to build up these relationships in the full light of self-knowledge. No one can really thrive in a wholly institutionalised environment or in a purely intellectual career. Personal attachments are necessary. Love is not the mere play thing of romantic dispositions but belongs to the realities of daily life where a loving word, touch or gesture goes a long way towards making us feel whole and satisfied.

The Power of Communication

In today's world, the power of communication is essential. At the same time, the art of conversation to have been forgotten and often people have reduced themselves to a limited vocabulary of monosyllables such as 'yeah', 'no', 'fine', 'ok', 'hi' and so on. The taciturn Englishmen, the voluble French, the inscrutable Chinese and the garrulous Indian— these are racial stereotypes that exist but as the world gets linked through the internet, both written and verbal, communication is essential. The power of communicating means expressing your thoughts and feelings effectively and putting your point of view across in a pleasant way. Whether it is business negotiations, international diplomacy or even a family interaction, it is important to put your viewpoint across pleasantly. Sometimes things are better left unsaid, but sometimes one may feel regret at not having expressed oneself adequately at the right time. To be Ms Malaprop is unfortunate and can have disastrous consequences as people are judged not only by their actions but by their words.

Improve Your Communication Skills

1. Children are encouraged to speak up in class, participate in debates and take up public speaking so that they learn communication skills early in life. Such exercises give you the ability to think on your feet and keep your wits about you.

2. Whenever you speak you are revealing something about your own personality and background. As Prof. Higgins in *My Fair Lady* would find out, your education, your place or country of origin, your status in society is unconsciously being expressed every time you speak. Your conversation will reveal to others whether you are kind or selfish, rude or polite, open minded or rigid, cheerful or morose, humorous or dour.

3. In order to say pleasing and tactful things which come across as being sincere, you have to cultivate such traits as alertness, kindness, tolerance, cheerfulness and an ability to appreciate another's point of view. People have so many hidden woes you never know when your words touch a sore spot. Hence cultivate kindness and be gentle in your speech.

4. A skillful communicator or conversationalist is one who has something to say, but his success lies in making others want to talk as well as to listen.

5. Communication does not mean a monologue in which one person monopolises the conversation.

6. Communication means the ability to draw out others into the conversation on topics of common interest.

7. 'Small talk' is a phrase which is used to denote that people exchange when they are getting acquainted or when they are thrown together for a few minutes of conversation. To be ready with such conversational fillers, you do not have to be blessed with unusual gifts. Feel a friendly interest in others without being pryingly inquisitive, notice what is going on around you, give yourself upto the enjoyment of the moment and you will never be tongue-tied.

8. Be a good listener and pay attention to what the other person is saying.

9. Use words effectively. Remember that the spoken word and the sprung arrow can never be taken back. Hurtful and unkind words stick in the mind, seemingly forever, especially in the case of children. A simple rule to follows is—if you can say something positive say it. Keep all harsh, biting, sarcastic and unkind words unsaid. There are many people such as mothers-in-law, critical bosses, overbearing parents and thoughtless spouses who would do well to exercise tongue control!

10. While some people talk too little because they are self-conscious and feel that they would say the wrong thing, that they remain silent to the point of appearing rude. Those who talk too much also do so because they are self-conscious. They chatter not because they have something to say but because they strive to be noticed. Don't be a compulsive attention seeker by constantly talking, particularly about yourself, your achievements, your children and your work. It is highly tedious for others.

11. Good talkers should not become bores by appointing themselves as the entertainer for a group of people. Conversation is a form of play, and like any play, there must be give and take. Do not turn it into a lecture or a solo performance and avoid becoming intoxicated by the sound of your own voice as this will result in people shunning you the next time they meet you.

12. Inattention, talking loudly, staring, interrupting, correcting and contradicting, arguing aggressively, telling long anecdotes, bragging about yourself, sneering at others and inquisitiveness constitute bad conversation and hence should be avoided.

The Theory of 'Instant'

Was it just a few generations back, that patience was considered a prized virtue to be cultivated over the years? Today's society is not for patient plodders. Rather, being the era of supersonic jets, satellites and computers, the key word is 'instant'. Everything is instant, from instant coffee and instant noodles to instant love, instant marriage, instant divorce, instant fame and instant riches. Life today is no longer short - in fact, longevity is a problem as the expectancy of life has gone up even in the developing nations, let alone in the West and in Japan, where the average life span is eighty years. Despite this reality, however, everyone is in a hurry. No one feels the need to space things out and savour life. Instead, everything must be now, at once, immediately, instantly. Psychologist and Reiki expert Paula Horan says 'these are days of quick trips, disposable diapers, throwaway morality, one-night stands, over weight bodies, and pills that do everything from cheer, to quite, to kill. It's a time when there is much in the show window, and nothing in the stockroom.'

In the past, relationships were meant to last a lifetime. Traditional Hindu belief has it that a man and a woman were joined together in holy wedlock over seven lifetimes. This concept is virtually obsolete today, with permanence, like patience, having little relevance in an instant lifestyle in which instant gratification is the order of the day. The underlying philosophy is that every individual should experience as much as possible in life. The chase and subtle nuances of a lengthy romance are out. There is no time for reams of long letters, with perhaps a sonnet or two in between. Such ideas went out with Elizabeth Barrett and Robert Browning.

Today it is all instant. Boy meets girl. Boy and girl fall in love. Money permitting, they wed as love literally rushes out of the door where there is poverty. The offspring follows shortly thereafter, often from a test-tube. Once the novelty wears off, bickering and domestic discord follow. Disharmony between the sexes is the order of the day. Why bother to persevere with a relationship which has lost its gloss?

Instant divorce follows. Move over. Make way for the next encounter, a new relationship, new sensations, a whole new experience.

As the generation of adults addicted to the 'instant' philosophy greys into old age, they will find themselves shunted into cold and soulless institutions, as there is no family member to care for them when they turn infirm. Money would have to buy them institutionalised care.

Thus, in the circle of life the wheel has turned a full circle and the philosophy of 'instant' has crept into our souls. With too much emphasis being placed on the present, on one's own pleasure, one's own identity and one's own material advancement, with little thought of a spirit of sacrifice for the family, of accommodation and tolerance, the future of this instant culture is invariably fraught with threats of violence, loneliness, alienation and finally even suicide. Disproving once again the old adage that 'no man is an island' human beings in this cultural ethos inevitably sit locked up alone in his or her own private hell. The human being has little ability to cope with problems single-handed. Communication and conversation has been side-tracked ever since television and videos entered the precincts of the home. Now instant communication specialists and analysts have sprouted in order to help the individual to discuss and overcome his or her problems and cope with the demons inside.

As in the case of instant human relations, instant food also brings in its wake its own problems. Hidden quantities of salt, sugar, chemical preservatives and colouring make packaged food a health hazard, with diseases such as high blood sugar, high blood pressure, coronary and respiratory complaints and even cancer being linked to a diet dependent on such foods. Doctors have found that children existing on a diet which has high amounts of sugar, fats and carbohydrates exhibit delinquent behaviour. Instant packeted foods are not a substitute for a balanced diet of fresh fruits, vegetables, proteins and carbohydrates.

A generation of television viewing, couch potatoes, channel surfing on their 'remotes' grows up ignorant of the harsh realities of life, which are not quite like those which are shown on the never ending 'soaps', With little guidance from parents, teachers or the church, not many youngsters are equipped to deal with setbacks, reverses and the trauma of illness. Many teenagers live alone and all too often, drugs, alcohol and crime are used as crutches to evade the realities of the problems at hand. Once again, the old proverbs that 'adversity maketh a man' and that 'suffering ennobles the soul' is meaningless for the instant generation. Young people see little sense in suffering endless pain or being hooked onto life support systems in hospitals, particularly for those who are terminally ill. The instant culture strives to seek new solutions to the problems of life and society, along with working on a new mindset to tackle the difficulties of present day existence. Compassion therefore was not a quality which was valued in this society.

Instant culture is not without its good points, especially in terms of technological advancement in all spheres of activity, such as internet, the fax and photocopying machines, cellular phones and the use of lasers in medicine. The need of the hour is to try to blend together the benefits of instant technology with the timeless human qualities of close family and friendship bonds, tolerance, compassion and non-violence. There has to be a conscious effort to eschew the seductive lure of a money-oriented consumer culture. Once acquired, wealth and possessions offer little lasting mental peace or satisfaction.

The entry of spiritual gurus who offer instant *nirvana* through the chanting of magical *mantras* are yet another aberration of the instant culture which seeks a short cut to contentment. The instant slimming pills, aerobics and exercise contraptions are another hoax perpetrated by this philosophy. Modern day eating disorders such as anorexia nervosa and bulimia are manifestations of a restless and rudderless generation which follows the dictates of fashion creators, blindly. The obsession with one's looks and figure and equating one's self worth with these has lead to the ruination of both health and mental balance.

The theory of instant, which is influencing too much of our present day lifestyles, needs to be closely examined and analysed so that one can pick the best of that which is traditional and that which is current or even futuristic. Human beings have been endowed with a brain and emotions. They cannot and should not become robots and automatons mindlessly following the herd. Instant fame, instant wealth and instant emotions are all too brief and the instant fall or letdown that invariably follows, brings in its wake feelings of rejection and insecurity. These feelings play havoc with a person's psyche and the ever-growing numbers who need to be treated for psychological disorders are proof that wealth, fame and possessions do not ensure mental well-being. Perhaps it is time to introspect,

and rationalise one's goals and expectations. Traditional values such as happiness, peace of mind and family ties, along with such qualities as patience, tolerance and self-restraint need to be cultivated instead of blindly groping for a materialistic, consumerist and instant lifestyle.

Curbing Materialistic Values

Don't keep up with the joneses

If one sits dawn to analyze the reasons for one's restlessness, unhappiness and anxiety one will find that discontent is at the bottom of it. Today very few bother to count their blessings and appreciate what they have. Everyone is looking around, seeking to acquire, grasp, accumulate and outdo others. In this quest for happiness, man feels happiness lies in chasing shadows of pleasures, possessions and power. Happiness actually lies in contentment and being loved as well as loving others. The philoshopy of the day seems to be 'If only I had more...'. A sticker at the back of a car states 'he who dies with the most toys, wins'.

Our clocks, notepads, utensils, clothes and crockery all carry the logos of the latest 'in products'. While our T-shirts parade their designers, or carry the logos of tobacco, soft drink or sports equipment. Our athletes are less worried about winning national or international laurels on the sports field. Rather once they become 'names' they are awarded commercial contracts to wear conspicuous brand-name labels. Entertainment anywhere is punctuated by advertisements. How can one concentrate when every segment of film or a sporting event telecast is sponsored by a product? India is no longer a country of spiritual values but one in which mammon worship and greed has led to innumerable girls being dowsed with kerosene because they failled to bring in a scooter, a television set, a fridge or a cash settlement.

Possessions have become our masters and we are slaves to them. Technology is pushing us into multiplying our needs. For example, the children are no longer content with books and marbles—they want their own rooms, computers, CD-Roms, laser toys, video games..., the list is endless and frightening. If we do not curb this desire for consumerism and keeping up with our neighbours in a game of materialistic oneupmanship, we are doomed to a life of unhappy discontent.

While it is true that we can no longer go back to the era of a loincloth, thatched roof and the Vedas, we must intelligently plan our lives so that consumerism does not consume us. Learn to say no, to do without and to live within your means. Do not be lured by the trap to spend more on your credit card so that you get a free gift and are then left frantically striving to earn more, by fair means or foul, to pay off your debtors.

While poverty is depressing, so is the mad scramble after wealth and material possessions. One should try to keep one's wants within reason and strike a right balance between earning enough for necessities and needs and not for greed. Since the dividing line between a man's need and greed is thin, unless he learns the virtue of contentment, desires can change and corrupt a person's outlook.

Indeed it gives us much to think about and strive to put into action. One should learn to want what one has rather than long to have what you want.

Don't Neglect the Children

The Indian social system has always placed a great emphasis on children—having them, providing for them, helping them to grow up, guiding them into careers and finally into marriage. In fact, having children and raising them was the raison d'etre of most people's lives. Today as the corrosive trends seep in from the west, there are DINK (double income, no kids) couples and many others who are pooh-poohing the obsession with children, saying that too much time, energy and, most of all, money goes into having children. In an article titled 'More expensive than a Porsche - Are children

worth the cradle?' Margarette Driscoll writes about the cost of raising children in England. In an indepth study entitled 'What price a child', consumer journalist Jan Walsh carried out a comprehensive survey commissioned by ASDA, the supermarket chain in England. 'Low cost' children on welfare or 46 per cent of two-parent families spent pounds 26,128 on their children by the time they are 21. Mr and Mrs Ordinary in their three-bedroom, semi-detached house spent pounds 100,000 while the snooties of Kensington spent pounds 295,000 on their children, inclusive of nannies and school fees. Today with the man, woman relationship in decline in the west and with so many marriages crumbling, children are low priority and hence their declining birth rate. They feel that children are not a worthwhile 'investment'.

In India, we are still natural enough to want marriage and children. After all the childless may have all the money, but they have only half the fun. The zeal to have children often comes in when it is already too late and when career satisfaction does not fulfill all that one craves for in life. Many westerners adopt children or opt to have children out of wedlock - the single mothers of the west try to emphasise that there is no need to have the support of a man. After having studied the effects of close to 50 years of high divorce rates in the west it is evident that a disturbed childhood results in disturbed adolescence and adults. There is really no substitute for a stable two-parent household.

The extremely callous attitude that parents can have toward their children is exemplified by the article 'Baby left on a pavement as parents dine in style in New York' in which a 14-month was left unattended on a New York pavement while the parents dined in style at a Manhatten restaurant. The parents were jailed for neglect but the mother Annette Sorenson, who hailed from Denmark, asserted that in Denmark it was quite common for children to be left unattended while their parents shopped or dined. The waiters had suggested that the couple opt for a larger table which could have accommodated the stroller but the couple declined!

Lest we complacently point fingers at others we would do well to remember the large number of children who got lost during the recent trade fair in Pragati Maidan as their parents shopped mindlessly! The reason

shootouts in England and America by deranged men with guns in schools and churches should serve as an eye opener to us.

In India also we have millions of street children who are victims of the worst type of exploitation and child abuse, drug addiction and child prostitution. Let the educated middle classes not add to these numbers by neglecting their children. Becoming a parent is a serious business which requires a sense of commitment and responsibility. Parenthood is not all drudgery - it gives you a great sense of security, of love, joy and hope. Parents are called upon to teach the children such timeless values as integrity, responsibility, loyalty and building up a value system which is your child's greatest asset as a future citizen. Their best moral compass is you and your spouse.

One of the biggest myths about parenting has been the 'buzzword' of 'quality time'. As far as babies are concerned, there is no such thing as quality time - it is just quantity as the child gets up, feeds, bathes, is put to sleep, wails, gets up and has to be fed and changed again. In order to convince women that they do justice to their jobs outside the home if they devote 'quality time' to their children is one of the many misleading concepts of today's generation. Were our mothers uneducated doormats to have spent all their time in raising children? An answer to this is to study the steady increase in juvenile crime rates and teenaged insecurities and abberative behaviour. As Swami Chinmayannanda once told and audience of ladies, 'children are not bad - mothers are, as they are more selfish and less devoted to their children than the previous generation. Ten minutes a week from a busy mother is certainly not what a baby deserves for growth.' Author and psychologist Ronal Levant asserts, 'children need vast amounts of parental time and attention. It is an illusion to think they are going to be on your time-table and that you can say `okay, we've got half-an-hour, lets get on with it".

Experts agree that many of the most important elements in the children's lives - regular routines and domestic rituals, consistency, the sense that their parents know and care about them - are exactly what is jettisoned when quality time substitutes for quantity time. Moreover kids do not shed their need for parental time when they become teenagers. At this stage they may get into drugs, bad company and feel reluctant to study, to subtly monitoring them is essential. When parents come home at 7.30 pm, and then head straight towards their fax machines and computers they are scarring the children by showing where their priorities lie. Neglected children show deviant behaviour and indiscipline in schools. They are crying for parental attention which they have not got due to work pressures on working parent.

A solution is to slowdown and take a break when you have children. If one is unwilling to put children before career, don't have them, as modern birth control methods make family planning a matter of personal choice and timing.

Also don't substitute neglect by overindulging them by giving them money and material possessions in lieu of your time and affection. A case in point is the lawlessness exhibited by 'rish brats' in our cities who have become role models for the poorer kids down the road. A major problem with these youngsters is that their prosperous parents are too busy with their business and socialising and leave raising of children to *ayahs*. They do not get the necessary guidance and values that must be instilled by the time the child is three or four. Child psychologist Gurmeet Kaur, who counsels children Delhi's elite schools, says 'in many cases where parent don't give time, I find the kids grow up with misshapen personalities, they are prone to violence if they don't get what they want.'

The absentee parents assuage guilt by giving the child anything they want. Love, discipline and time is essential for child rearing. Substituting these by giving the child unlimited money, fast cars, guns and a licence to do as they please is asking for trouble as children will then not obey the law and will expect their parents to bail them out when they are in trouble.

Some parenting tips

1. Low marks in school does not necessarily mean that the child has not made an effort. Both Einstein and Bill Gates did not excel in school.
2. Emotionally loaded and unkind words or cutting remarks scar the child.
3. Leniency does not necessarily make a child 'soft' but may make him more

responsible in the future. Harshness should not be equated with being a good parent.

4. Discipline the child judiciously, consistently and never in anger.

5. Don't swamp your child advice - it is boring and may cause him to revolt.

6. Do not go on comparing your child with other 'good' children as this will only make him feel jealousy and rivalry.

7. Do not scold the child or point out his shortcomings in front of teachers, friends or relatives. Remember that children have feelings and they should not be hurt by your insensitive conduct.

8. Do not nag children about their studies. The curriculum in our country is so overloaded that children suffer from 'burnout' right from class X. Parental nagging just adds to child's woes and will not ensure success.

9. Today's parent should neither by authoritarian nor too indulgent and permissive. Children need to be guided to be democratic in approach. Deal with your child coolly and in a mature fashion and encourage the child to express his opinions but also help him to recognise his responsibilities. Children brought up in a democratic manner tend to be socially responsible, self-confident, able to control aggression and have high self-esteem. They are also able to make social and personal adjustments easily.

10. Due to the overloaded curriculum and competitive environment our children have to sacrifice their childhood at the altar of studies and academic achievement. Until this system is modified, never grudge them their playing time as play is therapeutic for children.

Take care of your children for they are your richest treasure and your greatest contribution to society.

Doing one's Duty-Caring for the Aged

Life is a duty: dare it!
Life is a burden: bear it!

The cultures of Asia have long had a veneration for elders and filial piety was considered one of the main duties of a householder in Confucian China. Indian culture also enjoins on us to look after the lederly and to be respectful towards them. In the joint family system, the elders had a special place as the head of the household.

In a unique experiment conducted by 26 year old Pat Moore in New York in 1985 who disguised herself as an 85 year old to see how the elderly were treated and the problems they faced. At the end of the day, she was angry because she had been 'condescended to, ignored, counted out... people, I felt, really judged a book by its cover.' During this experiment, she was mugged and robbed and dealt with rudely. The entire experiment was a revelation of how the elderly could be ill-treated but there were also some instances of people being kind and helpful.

In view of the large segments of the greying population in the world, we must do our duty towards our elders. The western world has its own set of values in which independence and individuality are the cornerstones of their society. They find it humiliating to be a 'burden' on their children and remain alone as long as possible. When they are no longer self-sufficient they are institutionalised by their children.

India too has witnessed a burgeoning of the elderly population and some states such a

Himachal Pradesh have made it mandatory by legislation to look after elders. It is a sad fact that what was once a part of our culture now needs to be legislated.

The break-up of the joint family, increasing urbanisation, children working abroad have all contributed towards the problems of the aged, e.g. 72 year old Laxmi Iyer is many miles apart from her only son. Mrs Iyer is alone in an old age home. My son takes good care of me and I am happy, she says. However, the expression on her face has a different story to tell. She showed all the signs of a neglected and lonely person. Hers is not an isolated instance. Another example are the homes of non-resident Indians in Tiruvalla in Kerala. The aged parents here struggle to cope with the problems of infirmity and loneliness. Most parents admit that though their children urge them to accompany them abroad, they are reluctant. Life there, according to them is even more lonely. All this has led to the sprouting up of old age homes all over the country. However studies have shown that most of the inmates in these homes suffer from depression.

Plan your old age

Retirement can come as a intimidating but welcome time. The days of living on your pension have gone. Instead one has to give careful thought and considerartion as to how and where one would spent their fragile years. Questions such as how will I take care of my monthly expenditure? What if my children view me a burden for the rest of my life? also cause increasing concern. To deal with all these questions, it is advisable to start planning early. Take the example of Mr Chari, aged 45. He has to provide for the education of his children, marry his daughter and buy his dream home. How should he go about it? One of the many options in front of him would be to invest

Rs 30,000 per annum for 15 years in PPF (self) or alternatively he could invest in UTI Child Gift Growth Funds of Rs 10,000 per annum for 20 years which will yield adequate funds for the education of his child. The point to be noted here that planning early always works to your advantage. Its not enough to save, you must invest and its not enough to invest but invest wisely. Once one has ascertained his needs, one can make planned investments. One should remember to take the money's maturity value and the time period of investment in consideration says Sushil Chandra Chopra. 'I always knew that Iwould'nt be able to manage in this money (pension). So I put my money in other instruments like life insurance schemes, fixed deposits, property, stocks and shares, and national savings certificates...' Senior citizens should ensure liquidity. Bank deposits serve this purpose.

Thus, the moral of the story is to plan 10-15 years ahead of your retirement. Otherwise you will see your living standards plummet, this would increase hardship dependence and depression.

The government on its part is trying to come up with a national policy for older persons. Some of its provisions are:

Policy proposals

Economic measures: A significant expansion in the ambit of the old age pension scheme for the poor, with the ultimate objective to cover all elderly persons below the poverty line.

- Revision at intervals of monthly pension and sensitivity in taxation policies with a view to ensuring that inflation does not deflate actual purchasing power.
- Tax-concessions including higher standard deduction and a son/daughter whose aged parents stay with them.

Health care: Affordable health services, heavily subsidised for the poor and with a graded system of user charges for others.

- Development of health insurance.
- Directives to public hospitals to ensure that elderly patients are not subjected to long waits and visits to different counters for medical tests and treatment.

Housing: Earmarking 10 per cent of houses/house sites under urban and rural housing schemes for lower-income segments for elderly persons.

- Easy access to loans for purchase of housing and major repairs.
- Special consideration in matters relating to transfer of property, and property tax.

Legal: Introduction of special provisions in the IPC to protect older persons from domestic violence and a machinery to attend to all such cases promptly.

- Review of tenancy legislation so that their rights of occupancy are restored speedily.

Special focus: To identify the more vulnerable among the aged-the disabled, the infirm, the chronically sick and those without family support, and provide welfare services to them on a priority basis.

- Institutional care only as a last resort when personal circumstances are such that staying in old age homes becomes absolutely necessary.

Implementation mechanism

- To ensure effective implementation the government plans to set up a National Council for Older Persons headed by the minister for Social Justice and Empowerment with representatives of relevant central ministries, the Planning Commission, NGOs, media and experts.
- Targets to be set within the framework of a time schedule.

Responsibility for implementation of action plans to be specified.

- Detailed review every three years.
- An autonomous National Association of Older Persons (NAOP) be set up to mobilise senior citizens, articulate their interests, promote programmes for their well-being and to advise the government on all matters relating to older persons.

Though this scheme may have several pitfalls, the experts point out that governmental effort can only supplement and not replace family support and caring for the elders. The elderly may appear to live in the past and may seem boring to you. It is only when you make an effort to talk to them that makes you realise how receptive they are to the changes around them.

The modernity in their thinking may come to you as a surprise. All of us feel the need to be wanted and loved. Elders too feel this need. Be sensitive towards them, take their advice and help and watch them grow. The youngsters often use the phrase 'you don't know anything' little realising how much this hurts the grandparents or parents. Always remember that they are the ones who taught you to speak in the first place.

Allow the older people to initiate their own decisions after considering the options.

Always involve them in decisions regarding their future.

Services which are usually available on payment are:

a) Home help—assistance with household tasks.

b) Trained nurses

In the case the situation makes it imperative to put the elderly in a home always check the following:

1. Does the home have diversional and physiotherapy programmes.
2. Do community groups visit
3. Are services from hairdressers, dentists, optometrists and podiatrists available.
4. Are the residents treated as individuals with courtesy and respect.
5. Are residents allowed to keep personal possessions, e.g. pictures.
6. Does the home cater to special diets.
7. Are the cooling systems adequate.
8. Is their a garden and an outdoor area.

However, always remember that putting them in an old age home is not the end of your duty. There are many sad instances of people in these homes who never have any visitors. Hence, make it a point to keep in touch by writing letters or sending e-mails. Visit your parents as frequently as possible. Remember you may be in the same boat one day.

However, the situation in India is not yet so bad. Have you heard of modern day joint families? Yes! Joint families are now being recast and remoulded to suit the modern day demands. The sheer difficulties of managing both the economic and domestic fronts have prompted younger generations to review the joint family system. The system that has evolved is a two-way one, where the younger generation has the comfort of knowing that they are well looked after, the elders feel more secure and will get moral and physical support in times of illness or just loneliness. However in this situation also, both sets should be given ample breathing space. Do not interfere too much or dictate terms in each other's lives to keep the system functioning smoothly, e.g. each unit takes care of its own day to day expenses - one may also have separate kitchens.

Thus the modern day joint family is a place where the youngsters can draw from the wealth of wisdom and experience of the elders and the latter can remain active by contributing their advice and guidance to the household. The grandchildren may also often shower more love than the children and this works wonderfully for the psyche of the old people.

How to Make Friends

Blood is no longer thicker than water. Changing patterns of life and urbanisation have necessitated close associations between people. Friends now do what family once did. They cook together, holiday together and even buy property together. They have become an essential support system in tragedy and celebration thus spawning its own custom and value system.

The new family is a family by choice and not just genes e.g. the Aligan family who are a group of 8 families living in a building called Aligan in Calcutta. This group functions as a joint family. All the rites of passage from birth till death are a group affair. Their exists a traditional division of labour between them. The process of urbanisation mutated joint families into extended families and extended families into nuclear units. Lost in big cities, these units are starved for company and companionship. They now look for new families and new moorings.

The institution of marriage has also undergone a change. Couples today have more equal relationships. The division of labour is clear-cut. Anthropologists point out that there is an absence of generalised exchange where one person may do more than the other. However there is tension in equality and hence couples need other couples. The increasing divorce rates and single parents also make friendship a valuable commodity. Friends are not as judgmental as the family, says Arpita, a 35 year old single parent.

Thus the new Indians make their friends through work, friendship and even common hobbies. With more income at their disposal, these new groups can even go out together or plan holidays together.

Here are a few ways in which you can start your 'new family' or in other words, make friends:

1. Smile and project a relaxed body language
2. Cultivate a genuine interest in people.
3. Make it a point to remember people's names.
4. Be a good listener.
5. Get over your fear and half the battle is won.
6. Start the conversation about general topics like the weather, work etc.
7. Make compliments sincerely.
8. Since everybody enjoys the opportunity to talk about themselves, allow the other person to talk.
9. Keep the conversation lively.
10. Avoid ignoring people.
11. Cultivate a good sense of humour.
12. Give the other person a feeling of importance.
13. Respect the other person's opinion.
14. Graciously end the conversation when you have nothing more to say.
15. Maintain contact.
16. Always remember that friendship is always around the corner but waiting for you to make the first move.

Home and Family as the Basic Unit of Society

The family is the primary social structure of human society and fulfills many needs which are indispensable for the continuity, the change, and the stability necessary for human existence. The family fulfils a multifarious and multi-dimensional role as it takes care of the emotional, physical and financial needs of human beings.

Traditionally, agrarian societies all over the world had a predominance of extended families. These families were generally patriarchal and authoritarian with all members being guided in their activities by an elder family head. Women, generally had a subordinate position and marriage was guided by rules of kinship rather than those of courtship. The family was an important unit of economic, cultural, religious and even political activity. The economic structure of such societies was closed and exposure to technology or mass media rare. Hence the total volume of knowledge in the form of mythology folklore and folk songs was handed down by the elder generation to the younger, by oral tradition. Primarily due to this reason, age was an important element governing status and privileges in such societies. Feelings of individuality and personal freedom was alien to this type of family structure.

Such a society existed in England and in Europe until the beginning of the Industrial Revolution.

The concept of the family as being nuclear is not an Indian concept, and family jointness continues to be a major sociological phenomenon in the Indian social structure.

By the term 'nuclear family' one denotes a couple and their unmarried children, but there are many variations, such as a supplemental nuclear family, in which widowed divorced or aged relative or relatives live together. Aged parents may also join one of their sons, or even daughters, to form an extended family. Nor can one state categorically that joint and nuclear families are either rural or urban as case studies have revealed that joint families predominate in even larger numbers in urban and semi-urban pockets. If the rural joint family stayed together because of agricultural and allied pursuits, the urban joint family may thrive due to a common family business, a profession, such as the legal or medical one, and due to common housing.

In its transition into modernity Indian society has been careful to preserve a great deal of that which is positive in its culture. The care, concern and sympathy for the aged, and for the very young, is widespread. Under this transition has evolved the 'new joint family' in which the older generation strives to be more accommodating and less authoritarian and lives in harmony with children and grand children.

The traditional joint family in which three or four generations lived under one roof had both its advantages and disadvantages. There was no feeling of alienation in the old and the needy. Children were brought up in an atmosphere of warmth and emotional stability. However this form of living together in an extended family situation called for a lot of mutual adjustment and consideration and resulted in a lack of individual initiative and freedom. Moreover, domestic strife due to competition and the unjust victimisation of the daughter-in-low for bringing inadequate dowry, are frequent in joint families and often lead to its disintegration.

Status is achieved, rather than ascribed, in an industrial society, and the isolated nuclear family is best suited for such a society. Moreover the nuclear family is able to achieve geographical mobility without being unduly tied down to a binding range of kin a obligations to them. In addition, a wide range of specialised institutions such as schools, hospitals, business firms and even the Church, Creches and the police step in to perform the duties earlier done by the family.

The 70's and 80's saw women stepping out of their homes in ever increasing numbers, not only to supplement the family income but also to fulfil their individual career aspirations. Without the support of kin, beyond that of the nuclear family, the conjugal bond is often strengthened and women are given a great deal of scope to exercise initiative, regain their individuality and remain independent.

However, some reservation has to be exercised in adopting the nuclear family as the ideal since this new family system has given rise to set problems and drawbacks in the relationships between the older and younger generation and between parents and children.

Since the nuclear family is a manifestation of the achievement-oriented, status conscious society, there is less time and energy for bestowing attention and care on individual members. The stresses and strains imposed on the individual is considerable, as it calls for a great deal of self-sufficiency, independence and self-reliance. Aged parents can no longer expect to depend financially on their sons who have to fulfil the demands of their own immediate family and social environment. With women working, and domestic help being scarce and unreliable, children are brought up in a more matter-of-fact and less loving style than the generations before. The creche and the nursery school are the modern-day substitutes for grandparents, aunts, uncles and a plethora of servants. Both at the creche and at the nursery school the infant faces competition and consequently has to build up resilience and toughness in order to cope with the pressures of the environment. The problems do not stop with childhood as younger children and adolescents often become victims of the 'latch-key syndrome' Each child has the house keys and after school is expected to return home, eat and study till their parents return in the evening. Returning to an empty house and remaining unsupervised for many house leads to loneliness, boredom and mindless viewing of the 'idiot box 'or television and endless hours on the computer and internet. Many teenagers find warmth and sympathy amongst peer groups or in casual relationships with the opposite sex.

What About the Position of Women?

Having achieved a measure of independence and initiative, and the freedom to pursue an individualist path, unfettered by the demands of the authoritarian older generation, is life a bed of roses for her? Perhaps not always so, for she is under severe pressure to achieve excellence in all roles—that of a home maker, a parent, a wife and a worker outside the home. The pace of this continuous pressure often results in psychosomatic stress ailments, tension and insecurity as doubts creep in as to whether she is indeed able to fulfil adequately the demands placed on her and juggle her multifarious roles to become 'superwoman'.

The modern man also is no longer monarch of all he surveys as his writ does not always run unchallenged on the domestic front. Not only is he expected to achieve success in his career but he also has to lend a hand to domestic chores, help out with children, and adjust to the schedule of his working wife. He can neither expect to be waited on hand at and foot, nor can he expect his decisions to be blindly accepted by his family, as that perhaps of his father and grand father were before him.

The compulsions of the nuclear family extract a certain response from its members and has a consequent impact on society.

The positive impact has been that men, women, and children have become more self-reliant, self possessed and independent. However in the absence of the cocoon of warmth and security which the joint family offered, there has been some unsettling repercussions such as neurosis, emotional instability, selfishness and excessive materialism. The preoccupation with success, achievement, status are western ideals which success, achievement, status are western ideals which seem worthy of emulation, but which once achieved often result in emptiness, loneliness and insecurity.

In the west, and indeed in some segments of our society, the nuclear family has yielded to its logical successor, the atomised family or the single parent family. The psychological and emotional scarring of the children of such families is too well-known to reiterate. An extreme concern with oneself, one's goals and aspirations detract from the general need to adjust and he sensitive to the needs of another. For all its infringements on personal liberty, the joint family offered a great deal of emotional and psychological sustenance which cannot be measured by any materialistic yardstick.

One can only conclude that so far the impact of the nuclear family on Indian society has not been unfavorable. But one would have to continuously guard against those aberrations of selfishness, greed, materialism and rigidity which crept into the western nuclear family to render it virtually obsolete today. Whereas it may be necessary for us to improve our social welfare system by having creches, old age homes and women's shelters, let not the existence of these institutions lead us to an attitude of indifference and irresponsibility to what must be our filial and social duties. We must not and do not want to reproduce western society with all its attendant problems of alienation depression, divorce, drug abuse and violence.

Be a Good Member of Society

We do live in our houses in isolation. We are part of a family, part of an apartment building, part of a society, part of a city. People often say how can one man make a difference? Of course, he or she can—did'nt Mahatma Gandhi, Swami Vivekananda and Mother Teresa move whole generations and countries? Apathy and indifference to our surroundings have made our cities into living hells, full of dirt and garbage. Everyone looks to another to clean up the mess. Look around you and at the end of everyday look at one action of yours that has been for someone other than yourself - your good deed for the day.

Some tips

1. We live in a multi-religious and multi-lingual society. Do not vitiate the atmosphere by making communal statements and derogatory comments about other communities.
2. Encourage your children to celebrate all festivals—Id, Diwali, Christmas and any other that they may want to.

3. Keep the environment clean. Do not litter, spit or urinate in public places. These habits and an absence of civic sense have made us highly unpopular when we go abroad, apart from the scathing comments from foreigners about the state of our cities.

4. Inculcate civic consciousness in children. The best way of doing this is to observe the correct norms yourself.

5. Do not get de-nationalised and forget our traditions of love, tolerance, patience and respect for elders. These should be passed on to the children through you rather than through the media.

6. Avoid adding to the corruption around us and do not bribe public servants if you are caught violating the rules. Pay the penalty instead.

7. Drive carefully and ensure that your car is finely tuned so that it is not adding to the air pollution.

8. Alert the authorities when there is traffic hazard on your road or if stray animals have become a nuisance.

9. Make sure that your name is included in the electoral role and make sure you vote during elections. There is no sense in grumbling about the state of affairs if one does not even bother to exercise ones franchise.

10. People avoid getting involved because they feel they will be victimised by the authorities. However, if one tackles all issues judiciously there is no reason why this should happen.

BESTSELLER

खुशहाल जीवन जीने के व्यावहारिक उपाय

निराशा छोड़ो सुख से जिओ

10 FUNDAMENTAL RULES of SUCCESS

No Stones Upturned

What's Your Emotional IQ

खुशी के 7 कदम

मन की उलझनें कैसे सुलझाएँ

आधुनिक जीवन शैली

The Success Failure

जीत निश्चित है!

Modern Letter Writing Course

HUMOROUS MIDDLES

SUCCESS 2020

How To Become a Successful Speaker & Presenter

Improve Your PRESENTATION SKILLS

SUCCESS THROUGH POSITIVE THINKING

Also Available in Hindi

Also Available in Hindi

Also Available in Kannada, Tamil

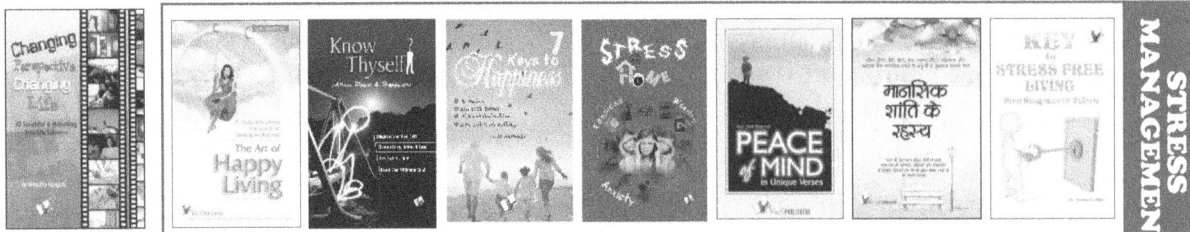

जीवन में सफल होने के उपाय

IMPROVE YOUR MEMORY POWER

MEMORY DEVELOPMENT COURSE

पर्सनैलिटी डेवेलपमेंट कोर्स

How to Become a Successful Manager

EXPLORE your Hidden Talents

EXPLORE YOUR POTENTIAL

WIN The battle of CONFLICTS WITHIN

Correct Manners & Etiquette

BESTSELLER

BODY Language

धैर्य एवं सहनशीलता

खुद से चर्चा का साक्षात्कार

भयमुक्त कैसे हों

व्यवहार कुशलता

आत्म-सम्मान

इम्प्रूव योर मेमोरी पॉवर IMPROVE YOUR MEMORY POWER

Group Discussion and Interview

Also Available in Kannada

PERFECT MAN

A Youngsters' Guide to PERSONALITY DEVELOPMENT

Build SELF-CONFIDENCE

हाँ, तुम एक विजेता हो

Woman's Guide to Personality Development

BE A WINNER

BESTSELLER

अपना व्यक्तित्व प्रभावशाली कैसे बनाएँ

Also Available in Kannada

Changing Perspective Changing Lives

The Art of Happy Living

Know Thyself

7 Keys to Happiness

STRESS

PEACE of MIND in Unique Verses

मानसिक शांति के रहस्य

KEY to STRESS FREE LIVING

All books available at www.vspublishers.com

RELIGION/SPIRITUALITY/ASTROLOGY/PALMISTRY/PALMISTRY/VASTU/HYPNOTISM

CAREER & BUSINESS MANAGEMENT

CHANAKYA

Chanakya Niti Kautilya Arthashastra

Also Available
in Hindi, Kannada

FIX Your PROBLEMS

MANAGE Your PROBLEMS

Also Available
in Hindi, Kannada

A Writer's Manual

A Complete Guide to Job Placement

VEDIC WISDOM

गीता ज्ञान

KNOW THE UPANISHADS

Dictionary of INDOLOGY

हिन्दुओं के व्रत, पर्व और तीज-त्योहार

धार्मिक सूक्तियाँ

भृगु संहिता फलित प्रकाश

HINDUISM Clarified & Simplified

Bhagavad Gita

HINDU

The Wisdom of the Gita

Krishna

BESTSELLER
मंत्र रहस्य

आओ ज्योतिष सीखें

BESTSELLER
PRACTICAL HYPNOTISM

PRACTICAL PALMISTRY

हस्तरेखा विज्ञान

Astrology for Layman

लाल किताब

NEW
अनिष्ट ग्रह ज्योतिष

Healing Power of GEMS and Stones

तांत्रिक सिद्धियाँ

Understanding

अंक ज्योतिष विज्ञान एवं भविष्यफल

Campus to CORPORATE

Out Of SYLLABUS

BEGINNERS' GUIDE TO JOURNALISM

Group Discussion

brain power

PREPARING INTERVIEW

SOCIAL NETWORKING

Benefits of Vaastu & Feng Shui

Public Speaking

WINNERS' PODIUM

Marketing for Beginners

Official Notings & Draftings

CAREER Planning

YOU ARE HIRED

Also Available in Kannada

हास्य कवि सम्मेलन

आओ हँस लो

प्रेरक प्रसंग

सिंहासन बत्तीसी

कबीर-चौरा

मजाक

चुटकुले

Rib-Tickling

MEDICAL JOKES & HUMOUR

Academic Jokes

Contact us at sales@vspublishers.com

QUIZ BOOKS

ENGLISH IMPROVEMENT

ACTIVITIES BOOK

QUOTES/SAYINGS

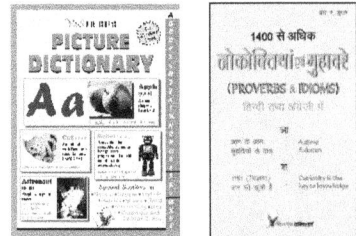

BIOGRAPHIES

CHILDREN SCIENCE LIBRARY

IELTS TECH

COMPUTER BOOKS

Also available in Hindi   Also available in Hindi

All books available at www.vspublishers.com

STUDENT DEVELOPMENT/LEARNING

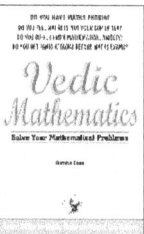

POPULAR SCIENCE

GREATEST CRAFTS & PROJECT for CHILDREN

WONDERS of the World

Ramayana

BESTSELLER
अच्छे अंकों से परीक्षा पास करने के 7 रहस्य

7 Mantras to Excel in EXAMS

71 Electrical & Electronic Projects

Children's SCIENCE ENCYCLOPEDIA

Also Available in Hindi

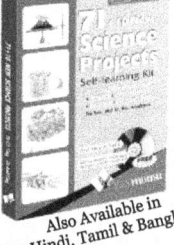

BESTSELLER
Super Student

आप भी मेरिट में आ सकते हैं

251 STUDY SECRETS

Vedic Mathematics
Solve Your Mathematical Problems

वैदिक गणित

NEW
71 + 10 New Mathematics Projects

Also Available in Hindi

Also Available in Hindi

Learning MATHEMATICS

वाद-विवाद (DEBATE)

निबन्ध संग्रह

Enhance Your Child's Talents

Poems for Children

The Science Projects Junior

71 Science Experiments

Also Available in Hindi

Also Available in Hindi

PUZZLES

MATHEMAGIC Puzzles & Brain Drainers

SUDOKU

SUDOKU

SUDOKU

Mind Benders Brain Teasers Puzzle Conundrums
150

101 + 10 New SCIENCE GAMES
Learning Science with Fun

71 Science Projects Self-Learning Kit

Also Available in Hindi

Also Available in Hindi, Tamil & Bangla

DRAWING BOOKS

ड्राइंग एण्ड पेंटिंग कोर्स

Drawing & Painting Course

Drawing & Painting Course

NEW
ड्रॉइंग कार्टून्स

NEW
DRAWING CARTOONS

The best of Science Funnies

71 + 10 Magic Tricks for Children

71 ARTS & CRAFTS FOR SCHOOL CHILDREN

CHILDREN'S ENCYCLOPEDIA – THE WORLD OF KNOWLEDGE

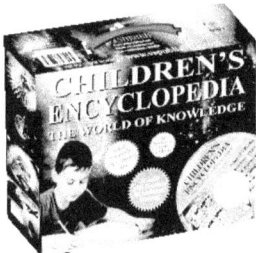

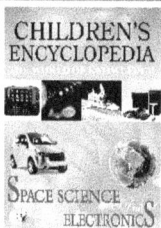

CHILDREN'S ENCYCLOPEDIA THE WORLD OF KNOWLEDGE

CHILDREN'S ENCYCLOPEDIA THE WORLD OF KNOWLEDGE
GENERAL KNOWLEDGE

CHILDREN'S ENCYCLOPEDIA THE WORLD OF KNOWLEDGE
LIFE SCIENCES & HUMAN BODY

CHILDREN'S ENCYCLOPEDIA
PHYSICS and CHEMISTRY

CHILDREN'S ENCYCLOPEDIA THE WORLD OF KNOWLEDGE
INVENTIONS & DISCOVERIES

CHILDREN'S ENCYCLOPEDIA
SPACE SCIENCE & ELECTRONICS

Contact us at sales@vspublishers.com

HINDI LITERATURE

MUSIC/MYSTERIES/MAGIC & FACT

TALES & STORIES

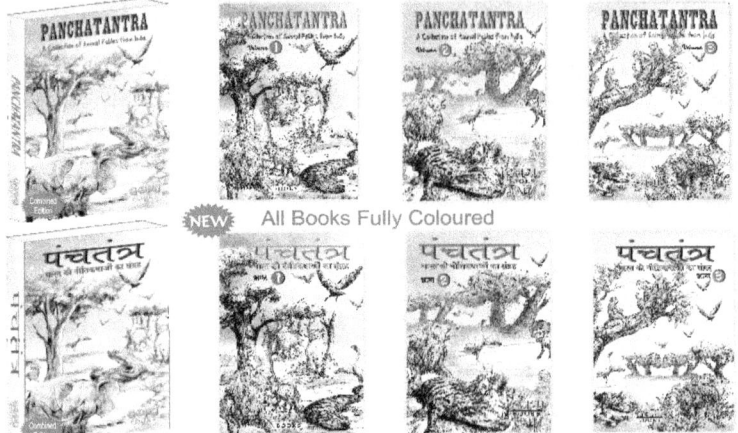

All Books Fully Coloured

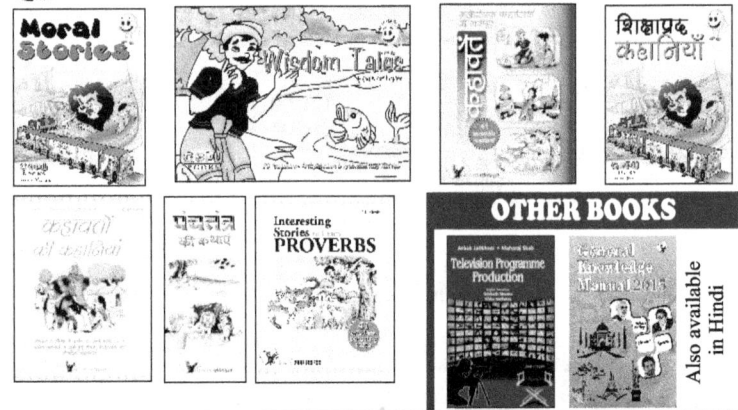

OTHER BOOKS

Also available in Hindi

CHILDREN TALES (बच्चों की कहानियाँ)

BANGLA LANGUAGE (बांगला भाषा)

www.ingramcontent.com/pod-product-compliance
Lightning Source LLC
Chambersburg PA
CBHW081339090426
42737CB00017B/3214